BASICS
FASHION DESIGN
06

Juliana Sissons

KNITWEAR

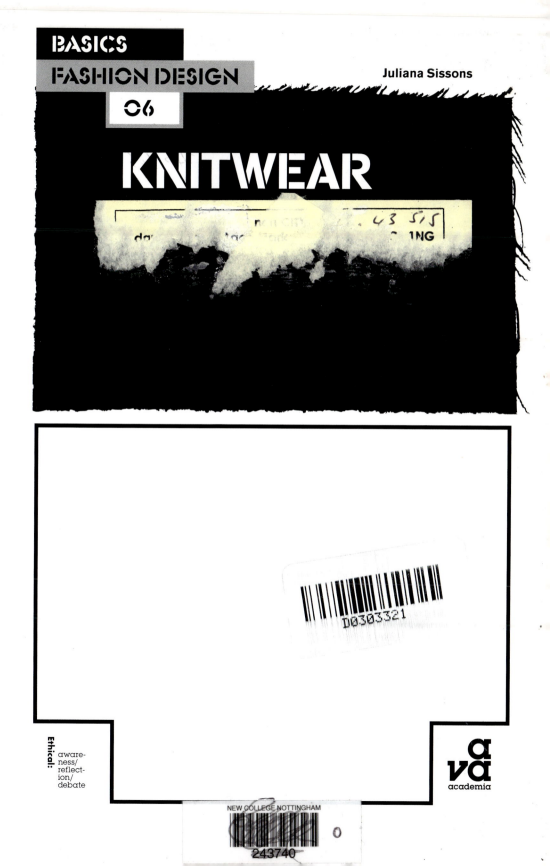

Ethical: aware-
ness/
reflect-
ion/
debate

ava
academia

An AVA Book

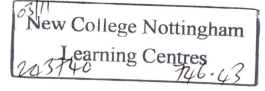

Published by AVA Publishing SA
Rue des Fontenailles 16
Case Postale
1000 Lausanne 6
Switzerland
Tel: +41 786 005 109
Email: enquiries@avabooks.com

Distributed by Thames & Hudson (ex-North America)
181a High Holborn
London WC1V 7QX
United Kingdom
Tel: +44 20 7845 5000
Fax: +44 20 7845 5055
Email: sales@thameshudson.co.uk
www.thamesandhudson.com

Distributed in the USA & Canada by:
Ingram Publisher Services Inc.
1 Ingram Blvd.
La Vergne TN 37086
USA
Tel: +1 866 400 5351
Fax: +1 800 838 1149
Email: customer.service@ingrampublisherservices.com

English Language Support Office
AVA Publishing (UK) Ltd.
Tel: +44 1903 204 455
Email: enquiries@avabooks.com

ISBN 978-2-940411-16-0

10 9 8 7 6 5 4 3 2 1

Design by Sifer Design

Production by AVA Book Production Pte. Ltd., Singapore
Tel: +65 6334 8173
Fax: +65 6259 9830
Email: production@avabooks.com.sg

All reasonable attempts have been made to trace, clear and credit the
copyright holders of the images reproduced in this book. However, if any
credits have been inadvertently omitted, the publisher will endeavour to
incorporate amendments in future editions.

1   Knitwear design by Johan Ku, part of his 'Emotional Sculpture' collection.

Contents

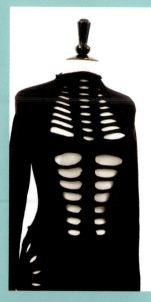

Contents

1   Knitwear design by Alexander
     McQueen, A/W09.

*'I reintroduced the idea of fine knitwear into fashion.
There's nothing more sexy than a twin set.'*

Vivienne Westwood

The machine knitting industry dates back to the early 16th
century, but it could not be more exciting and alive than it is
today. Knitting provides endless creative outcomes, enabling
an independent and experimental approach to design. Modern
developments in technology and manufacturing, coupled
with contemporary treatments and spinning technology,
have revived the knitwear industry. Knitwear can be found
at all levels of the fashion market, from the industrial mass
production of hosiery, underwear and sports wear to the use
of its sculptural qualities in high fashion and accessories, such
as bags, shoes and jewellery. The medium also provides an
astounding range of possibilities for art, interior design and
architecture.

Basics Fashion Design: Knitwear begins with a brief history
of knitting and knitwear design and an introduction to yarns,
fibres, machinery and tools. The book then leads you through
the essential stages of creative design development, with
a number of project briefs and practical skills: how to knit a
tension swatch; basic techniques on domestic machines and
how to create knitting patterns. It looks at the differences
between two- and three-dimensional design, exploring the
textural and sculptural qualities of knit. The final chapter
examines details and trims, from embellishment to fastenings.
In addition, *Basics Fashion Design: Knitwear* is richly
illustrated with the very best of contemporary knitwear design.
I hope that it will provide you with the fundamental skills,
knowledge and inspiration to design and create your own
innovative knitted textiles.

'It is a freedom to be able to make your own fabric
while working. For me it is the absolute challenge.'

Sandra Backlund

1   Blooms by Laura Wooding. Laura
recreated the volume and softness
of densely packed flowering blooms
using macramé and domestic knitting
techniques with lambswool yarns.

In order to take a fresh look at knitting, and at ideas that
are normally taken for granted, we should first understand
historically how these techniques came about and consider
the classic, timeless designs as significant and creative
starting points for further design development. Hand-
knitting skills and patterns have long been passed from
generation to generation, allowing a greater understanding
and acknowledgement of knitting as an intellectual, artistic
tradition. A growing number of new and exciting designers are
graduating each year from fashion and textile courses and, by
comparing their designs with the work from the early knitters, a
story starts to emerge.

This chapter offers an introduction to knit and knitwear
design, comparing traditional knitting techniques with their
modern reinventions. It looks at the characteristics and
behaviour of different yarns and fibres, from the traditional
to the contemporary, such as metallic, steel and plastic. It
offers an overview of knitting machines and tools, and the
different aspects of work that can be produced. Finally, it looks
at how developments in design and technology are radically
reinventing this traditional craft.

Reinventing traditional knitting

Developments in technology enable new ways of creating knitwear and knitted textiles, but many students and designers are looking to traditional techniques to inspire them and merge with contemporary ideas. Designers are capitalising on the unique qualities that knit has to offer, pushing boundaries with unusual yarns and materials and playing with scale. There is a natural interplay between craft, design and new technology. We will look at some of these traditional knits – fishermen's ganseys, Aran cables, Fair Isle and lace – and explore their modern reinventions.

A brief history

Wool fabric has protected us since the very early days and people may well have knitted, using only the fingers, as long ago as 1000BC. Techniques using circular peg frames, similar to French bobbin knitting, were also probably practised alongside hand pin knitting.

There are various European paintings that portray the Virgin Mary knitting, providing evidence that knitting was practised as early as the 14th century. Shown here is Master Bertram's painting of the Madonna, who is seen knitting Christ's seamless garment on four needles. Hand-knitting was commonplace in medieval Europe and the production of caps, gloves and socks was an important industry.

In 1589, the Reverend William Lee invented the stocking knitting frame, which was to revolutionise the knitwear trade. Initially created for use with the short, fine sheep's wool from Sherwood Forest, this first machine produced coarse knitting for peasant hose. Lee was unsuccessful in promoting the frame; Queen Elizabeth refused the patent because she feared that it would jeopardise the hand-knitting industry. He then developed the frame to be used with silk: the original machines had eight needles per inch; this new machine was thought to have 20 needles per inch and it was perfect for making expensive, fancy stockings. The English were still not interested and Lee took the

frame to France, where the machine eventually proved to be successful. By the end of the 17th century it was in increasingly extensive use across Europe. Knitting had become faster, because now, instead of knitting one stitch at a time, whole rows could be knitted at once. The machine was gradually refined further and by the 18th century the idea of knitting holes opened up new scope for design. By the late 19th century the knitwear industry was huge; new innovations in technology paved the way for the straight bar, flat frame.

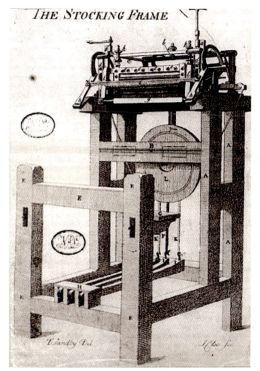

THE STOCKING FRAME

1   *Visit of the Angel*, known more
     commonly as the Knitting Madonna,
     by Master Bertram of Minden,
     1400–10.
2   The framework knitting machine was
     invented by William Lee in 1589.   2

Jerseys and guernseys

Jerseys and guernseys originate from the Channel Islands, just off the north coast of France. These fishermen's garments were hard-wearing, comfortable and warm; they were knitted in oiled wool with a tight stitch and could resist rain and sea spray. Original jerseys and guernseys were dark blue, almost black in colour, and were knitted in the round, using four or more needles, in order to secure a seamless garment. Designs were often knitted in banded patterns, sometimes displaying different textures between the bands.

Thanks to the opening up of trade routes in the 17th century, these garments soon became the fisherman's staple around the UK, where they were adapted with new patterns and textures (and are often referred to elsewhere as 'ganseys'). Stitches were passed down from generation to generation. The wealth of pattern in the stitches gave great scope for individual design. These garments were cherished, looked after, mended and often handed down. It is thought that a fisherman who died at sea could be identified by the handiwork of his guernsey.

1

Aran

The Aran Islands are located off the west coast of Ireland. Most historians agree that the Aran jumper is a relatively recent invention. The Irish government set up an initiative in the 1890s to encourage poorer families to weave and knit garments to sell.

The garments were originally knitted in thick, untreated wool, which retained its natural oils; they were mostly cream, but sometimes black in colour. An Aran knit is heavily patterned with closely knitted cables, honeycombs, diamonds and lattice effects; it quite often displays different patterning on the front and back. The basis of many Aran patterns is the simple cable, a twisted rope design, which consists of a certain number of stitches that are divided so they can be twisted around each other. A typical Aran design consists of a centre panel with two side panels and cable stitches. The knitter uses tools to move one stitch or a group of stitches over or behind another.

3

1   Shetland fishermen wearing
    individually patterned hand-knitted
    ganseys in worsted yarn, circa 1900.
    Shetland Museum and Archives.
2   Mini ganseys by Annie Shaw.
3   Modern interpretation of the traditional
    Aran knit by Alexander McQueen,
    A/W 2006.

Fair Isle

Fair Isle knitwear is known for its multicoloured, specialised patterns. Fair Isle, a tiny island south of the Shetlands, was a frequently visited trading centre for fleets coming from the north and Baltic seas. Influences from places such as Scandinavia and Spain can be seen in the Fair Isle knit.

Cottage industries flourished and continued to thrive until a decline in the early 1800s. By 1910 Fair Isle knitting had become popular again; knitters continued to experiment with patterns and colours and by the 1920s, the style had become a distinctive fashion for the wealthy and the middle classes.

While Aran knitting combines textured effects, Fair Isle knitting concentrates on pattern and colour. Fair Isle knitting is a combination of design repeats and motifs, which tend to be broken up into vertical or horizontal bands or blocks. Knitting instructions are taken from charts, which give a visual impression of how the design will look when finished. There is great design potential with the different combinations of border patterns and motifs. See more about Fair Isle patterns on pages 92–93.

2   3

Lace knitting

The Shetland Islands are also famous for their lace patterns, knitted in very fine, soft yarns. Lace shawls were worked from the outside edges in. Designs varied from quite simple mesh patterns, based on garter stitch, to intricate lace patterns, based on stocking stitch. Different lace patterns were given names to describe the stitch. Some had meanings, such as 'Old Shale', which depicted waves on the beach. Others were more descriptive, such as 'Feather and fan', 'Crest of the wave', 'Cat's paw' and 'Horseshoe'.

Lace patterns were capable of numerous modifications and combinations. This enabled the production of lace pieces that were luxurious to wear and individual in design. Lace knitting has never died out completely; many crafts people are still enjoying the challenge today. See pages 76–79 for more on lace.

Argyle patterned hose

Originating in Scotland, argyle stockings were traditionally worn with kilts, particularly by military regiments. The pattern was worked either in a large check, showing light, dark and a half-toned area between; or checked like tartan. Rather than being knitted in the round with four needles, these stockings were knitted on two needles with separate lengths of yarn for each colour.

1   Fair Isle knit by Hannah Taylor.
      Photography by Jojo Ma.
2   Shetland women knitting lace (left)
      and Fair Isle (right), early 20th century.
      Shetland Museum and Archives.
3   Modern interpretation of argyle
      stockings by Vivienne Westwood,
      A/W07. Catwalking.com.

Yarns and fibres

Your choice of yarns is very important and there are lots of factors to take into consideration; the most important being quality and suitability for the end result. Here we take a brief look at some of the many different yarns available to machine knitters and try to unravel some of the confusion over yarn thickness, the spinning process and the different types of fibre content.

All yarns are made from natural or man-made fibres, which come in various lengths known as 'filament' and 'staple'. Filaments are very long fibres, which are made in one continuous length. Synthetic fibres are produced in a filament form. They are often then cut into shorter staple lengths before being spun into yarn. The only natural filament fibre is silk. Staple fibres are much shorter in length: lots of separate pieces are twisted and spun together to make a staple yarn. Sometimes, for reasons of strength, design or economy, yarns can be made from a blend of staple and filament fibres.

Spinning

Spinning involves the twisting together of staple fibres to form lengths of yarn. A process called carding is first used to separate the entangled fibres. Carding machines, which consist of large rollers covered with sharp wires, create a thin blanket of fibres and these are divided into narrow strips, known as slubbings. The slubbings are then drawn out and spun. Yarn may be twisted in a clockwise or anti-clockwise direction, resulting in an 's' or 'z' twist. The yarn may be tightly twisted, producing a hard, strong yarn; or it can be lightly twisted, giving a bulky, soft yarn with less strength, but good insulating properties.

Hand-spun yarns can be machine-knitted, but are usually best suited to a chunky machine due to the uneven texture of the yarn. Single strand or 'ply' yarns are produced through the spinning process. These strands can be twisted together with other strands to produce thicker yarns. These yarns are known as two-ply, three-ply and so on. Plying also prevents yarn from twisting back on itself and makes the final knitting lie straighter. According to the number of single ends that have been combined, and the way the yarns are doubled, many different effects can be achieved. Fancy yarns have a variety of textures and colour blends applied at the spinning stage.

1–2 Selection of knitted swatches and hand-spun yarns by Jennifer Dalby.

2

Natural yarns

Natural yarns may be derived from animal or vegetable sources. The main three animal-based yarns are wool, hair and silk. The most common vegetable-based yarns are linen and cotton.

#28 Handspun Grey Blue Faced Leicester and Herdwick (chunky) yarn.

Hand knitted ladder stitch with natural rope.

1

Wool

Taken from the fleece of a sheep, wool is by far the most common type of yarn used in knitting. It has a natural elasticity, which makes it easy to work with. It can be chunky or fine, depending on the way it is spun and the quality can vary depending on the type of sheep. Some wool has a longer and thinner staple length; for example, merino wool, from the merino sheep, has a finer fibre than other wools. Shetland yarn has a shorter staple length; it is sometimes itchy because the shorter, thicker fibres poke out of the spun yarn. Worsted wool is spun with a mix of varying length fibres, making it smoother, stronger and more lustrous than Shetland wool.

Hair

Hair is taken from the coats of animals other than sheep, although hair fibres are often blended with sheep's wool. Examples include mohair, which comes from the angora goat. This is a luxury yarn with a unique hairy surface; when blended with wool or silk the appearance becomes more refined. Angora, which comes from the angora rabbit, is a soft, fluffy yarn. It is usually blended with wool to give it strength. Cashmere is another luxury yarn. Taken from the cashmere goat, this is a soft, warm and lightweight yarn.

Silk

Harvested from silkworms, silk is the only natural filament fibre and it is expensive. It is strong, with a smooth, shiny appearance and is often blended with other fibres to make it more versatile. Spun silk is cheaper, as it is made from the broken pieces of waste filament spun together. Wild silk, which is harvested from undomesticated silkworms, is coarse and uneven.

Linen

Linen's long staple fibres are taken from the stem of the flax plant. This strong yarn is lacking in elasticity and is often blended with other fibres, such as cotton, to make it easier to work with. Yarns are usually slubbed.

Cotton

Cotton is made from staple fibres of the cotton plant. This is also a strong, non-elastic yarn with a soft finish. Untreated cottons are more difficult to knit than mercerised cottons, which have a treatment added at the production stage.

1   Hand-knitted swatch, featuring ladder stitch with natural rope and hand-spun yarn, by Jennifer Dalby.

2   Selection of hand-knitted cable swatches by Jennifer Dalby, using her own hand-spun yarns and natural rope.

#25 Handspun Blue Faced Leicester, Falkland and Black Welsh Mountain yarn. Garment development sample.

#14 Handspun Swaledale yarn. Hand knitted large woven cable pattern.

#40 Handspun Herdwick yarn. Handknitted 6 cable stitch with natural rope.

Man-made yarns

The development of manufactured
fibres and their texturing processes
have inspired the knitting industry
and they have been beneficial in
many ways: they are easy and
inexpensive to produce and can be
blended with natural fibres that are
too fragile to use alone. However,
there are environmental drawbacks
as the entire production of these
yarns involves the chemical treatment
of raw materials and the use of coal
and oil. Definitions between natural
and man-made fibres are becoming
blurred as many natural fibres, such
as cotton, wool and flax, are regularly
subjected to chemical treatments.

Manufactured fibres fall into one of
two categories: regenerated and
synthetic. Regenerated fibres are
derived from natural substances,
such as wood pulp cellulose or milk.
Rayon, the best known of these, is
usually characterised by its sheen
and often used as a substitute for
silk. Viscose and acetate are both
products of the rayon family and
are all liable to melt under a hot iron.
Synthetic fibres, such as acrylic,
are made from petroleum-based
chemicals, plastic and/or coal.
Acrylic crimped fibre yarn is often
used as a wool substitute, but it is
less durable, not as warm and has
a tendency to stretch. Nylon is
another synthetic yarn: it is very
strong, non-absorbent and best
blended with wool. Polyester is
similar to nylon but with less shine.

Other man-made yarns include
metallic threads, such as Lurex,
which are made from aluminium and
coated in plastic. Manufacturing
of man-made yarns continues to
evolve and a great number of refined,
sophisticated yarns are available
today. There are now extremely fine
micro-fibres, which have opened
up new possibilities in the design of
yarns; stretch yarns are increasingly
being used in seamless garments
and new blends and textures are
continually being developed.

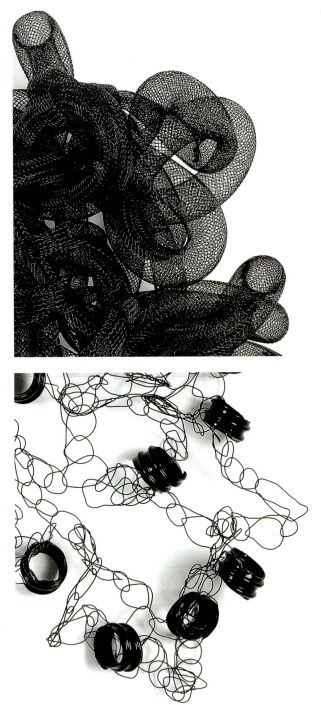

1

2

1–4 Selection of swatches by Victoria Hill, constructed using unusual, man-made yarns such as rubber, acrylic and wire.

3

4

Innovative yarns

Unusual effects in yarns are achieved by playing with colour, texture and heat settings. These effects can be added at the fibre, spinning or doubling stage. For example, a blend yarn has had different colours mixed together at fibre stage. A marl yarn is made up of two woollen spun single ends, in different colours, twisted together. It can also be called a twist or a 'granderelle' yarn. Nepp yarn has flecks of colour along its length, like tiny coloured balls of wool.

Buying yarns

Many companies specialise in selling yarns to the machine knitter. Industrial coned yarns are more commonly used by machine knitters; balled yarns are usually too expensive, tangle more often and don't go as far. However, it is a good idea to have a variety of unusual yarns for experimentation and small amounts of thicker yarns are useful for weaving in by hand.

1   Knit in chunky wool yarn by Alexander McQueen A/W09.
2   Different types of yarn (from top to bottom): fancy; woollen spun; Lurex; chenille; tape/ribbon; lace tape; bouclé; snarl; marl; twist; mohair; space-dyed crepe; slub; twisted Lurex; eyelash; slub.

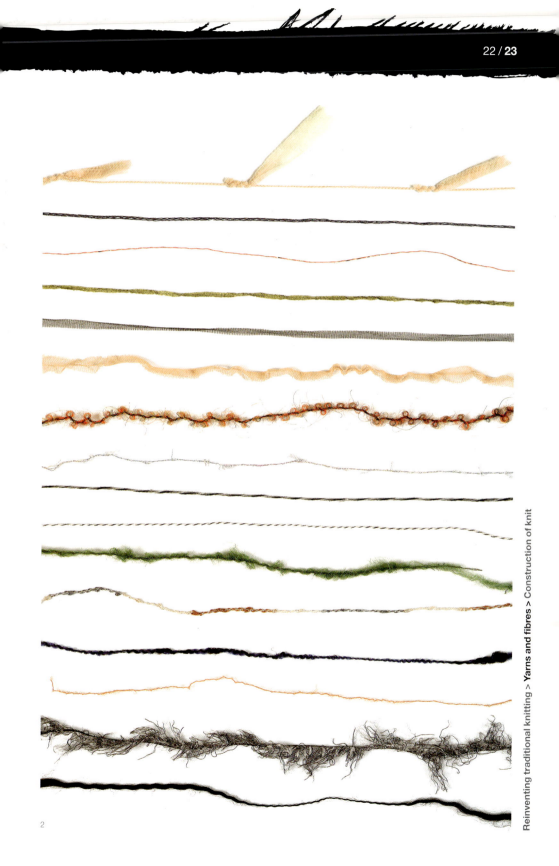

1   Dye tests by Georgia Northcoombs.
2   Jacket and mini-dress by Jessica
     Gaydon, dress (underneath) by Orla
     Savage. Photography by Jojo Ma.

Dyeing yarns

Exploring different effects with dye can give your work a unique feel and open up new design possibilities. Original base colours will affect the look of the final dyed colours, so use natural and light shades of yarn for the best results. Before dyeing, the yarn needs to be unravelled from the cone and wound into a skein (do this by winding it round the back of a chair) and tied together loosely, to avoid tangling. The yarn should also be washed to remove coatings.

Dylon dyes

Available from most hardware stores, Dylon dyes come in a wide range of colours. Each tin contains enough powder to dye approximately 227g (8oz) of yarn, although you can vary the amount of dye depending on the depth of shade required. It is a good idea to make a note of the amount of dye added to the weight of yarn and keep it with the yarn sample. These dyes are easy to use and come with full instructions. However, they do not work well with some synthetic yarns.

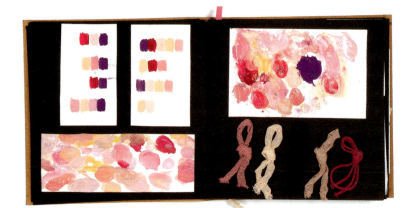

1

Acid dyes

These chemical dyes are strong and bright and have excellent colour fastness. They come in a powder form and require a similar dyeing process to the Dylon dyes. Only a few base colours are needed to create a whole range of colours. Two or more colours can be mixed and many shades can be created from one colour by varying the amount of dye used. When experimenting with these mixtures it is important to keep records of the amounts used in combination, together with a sample of the yarn before and after; for example, 30g wool yarn, red 40ml/blue 60ml. This information will serve as a useful starting point for new variations on the shade.

Vegetable dyes

Vegetable dyes can produce a beautiful range of colours but they tend not to be very strong and are also more likely to fade when washed. However, this is a cheaper way of dyeing yarns and the colours have inspired many soft, vintage-style collections. Dyes from gathered plant materials can provide interesting colour projects. They can also present a challenge when trying to replicate exact colours.

Space dyes

Space-dyed yarns are made up of a range of colours in one strand. This partial dyeing technique involves one skein being dipped in separate coloured dyes. Knitting these yarns in stripes and patterns creates unusual rainbow effects. Multicoloured Fair Isle patterns can also be created without having to change yarns.

2

Construction of knit

The basic structure of knit is a series of loops, created using one of two very different techniques: weft knitting and warp knitting. Weft knitting, the more common of the two, is the formation of loops using one continuous yarn, over successive courses throughout the length; the wales are perpendicular to the courses (see illustration 3). Warp knitting requires different machinery and involves lots of different yarns, one yarn per wale. This fabric has less stretch and is more difficult to unravel than weft knitting.

1

2

Stitch formation

On a knitting machine, the needles consist of two parts: the latch, hook and butt (see illustration 4). The stitch is in the hook; when the hook slides forwards, the existing stitch moves behind the latch. The yarn is then placed over the hook and as the needle slides back, the latch closes. A new stitch is formed when the existing stitch is pushed over the latch (see illustration 5).

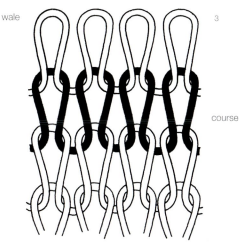

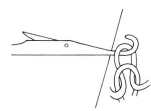 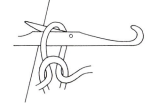

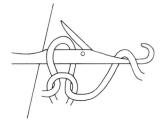

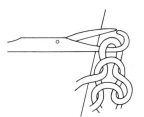

1   The simple wooden knitting wheel has provided many children with a basic knitting frame and an introduction to knit. Known as French knitting, the technique involves wrapping a narrow circular cord around the nails, to make a row, then passing the yarn behind the nails, forming two rows. By lifting the first row over the top of the second a stitch is formed, leaving one row on the nails. The knitting begins to form a tube through the centre of the reel.

2   A knitting machine showing a knitted piece in progress.

3   The diagram illustrates the structure of knit, showing the course (row) and the wale (stitch).

4   Machine needles feature a latch, a hook and a butt.

5   Series of diagrams showing how stitches are formed on a knitting machine.

Yarns and fibres > Construction of knit > Developments in design and technology

Machine basics

1   A standard gauge, single bed knitting machine, such as this one, is best for beginners.
2   A standard carriage for the Knitmaster knitting machine. A different carriage is needed for a double bed and is provided with the ribber. There are also many special carriages available for making lace and intarsia.

Knitting machines fall into two categories: single bed, with one set of needles; and double bed, with two sets of opposing needles. Most beginners buy a standard gauge, single bed machine, which produces a basic, stocking-stitch single fabric. It is simpler to start with a single bed machine as the needle positions are easier to understand and, as the knitting is visible, it is easier to repair mistakes. Single beds can also be used to produce mock ribs but these are not as professional as ribs made on a double bed. Most domestic machines have a punch card facility for patterning. Once you have got used to the single bed you can use a ribber attachment to convert it into a double bed machine. Having two needle beds offers more flexibility. The double bed can be used to produce a double knit or rib fabric and there are a huge number of stitch variations. Most manufacturers supply ribbers as accessories for their different models.

Tension

The yarn flow is controlled by a mast, tension spring and tension disc. As the tension is controlled mechanically the fabric quantity becomes more regular.

Machine bed

The bed holds the machine needles; these are latch hook needles, which enable the machine to swiftly pick up new stitches and drop off old ones.

1

The carriage

The carriage is moved across the bed and simply slides the needles forward in order to knit. Levers on top of the carriage control cams and can be used to select needles for a variety of stitches such as tuck and slip. Stitch size can be fine-tuned by adjusting the yarn tension in combination with the stitch size dial on the carriage.

Needle size / stitch gauge

The stitch gauge refers to the number of needles per inch across the needle bed. Different thicknesses of yarn can be used depending on the gauge of machine. Fine-gauge machines (7g) hold 250 needles and are suitable for knitting fine- to medium-weight yarns. Standard gauge (5g) machines hold 200 needles and are suitable for medium-weight yarns. Chunky gauge (3g) machines hold 100 needles and can accommodate thick, chunky yarns. It is possible to explore different yarn thicknesses on each of these gauges by knitting on every other needle (half-gauging the machine).

2

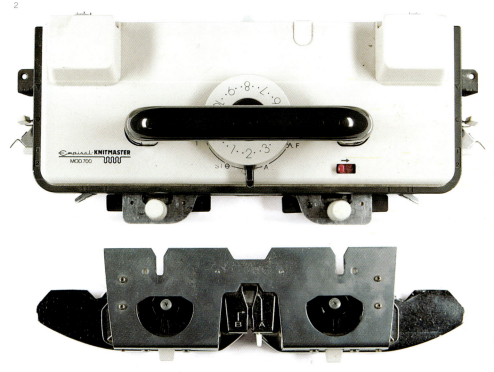

Machine types

The following is an overview of the three main types of knitting machine. Second-hand domestic machines are ideal for students and are widely available, either from dealers or from auction sites. Most models are equally reliable and roughly the same in price, except fine-gauge machines, which are sought after and usually more expensive.

Electronic machines

Electronic machines have a built-in programming capacity. Some machines use Mylar sheets to create the patterns, which can be repeated, reversed, knitted upside down, mirror imaged or doubled in length and width. If you are buying an electronic machine it is a good idea to consider a model that is compatible with a CAD/CAM program for knitwear, such as DesignaKnit.

1

2

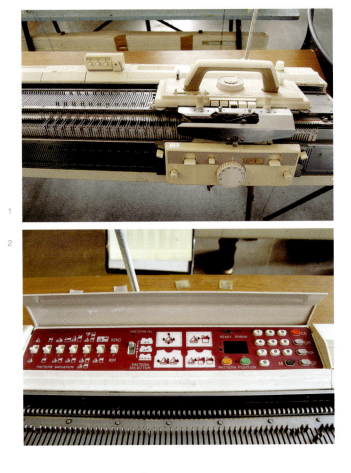

Hand-operated industrial machines

Hand-operated industrial machines are incredibly versatile; these machines have two fixed beds and are known as V-beds (from the side view they look like an inverted V). The beds are equally positioned in angle, which allows the knit to be equally weighted. They also have a greater range of gauges, offering the opportunity to experiment with very fine knit on gauges of 10 and 12. Tension can be altered for different parts of a garment, such as a rib border, full cardigan stitch knit and jersey stitch knit.

Electronic industrial machines

Today's automatic, electronically programmed machines are highly sophisticated. Some have four needle beds, allowing greater possibilities with shape. They can be used to knit different weights of yarn without having to change needle sizes. The latest machines produce complete garments without seams and with only one thread to sew in at the end, eliminating hand-finishing costs. The body and sleeves can be knitted at the same time, via a tubular knitting technique. Ribs, cuffs and hems can be knitted at the start, necklines at the end. The complete garment machines and programming systems are extremely expensive, having taken years of research and development to perfect; highly skilled sample technicians are required to operate them. The two main models offering the complete garment system are Shima Seiki of Japan and Stoll of Germany (although China is fast developing its machine-building industry).

3

4

1	Brother double bed punch card knitting machine.
2	Brother electronic machine.
3	Dubied hand-operated industrial machine.
4	Stoll electronic industrial machine.

Tools

Most machines will come with a selection of basic tools that are compatible with the gauge of the machine. These tools can be used on different machines as long as the gauges are the same.

The most useful tools are those used for selecting, moving, holding and repairing stitches. Using the right tools for manoeuvres such as creating lace holes and manual patterns, increasing and decreasing stitches and casting off, will not only save time but also make the task easier.

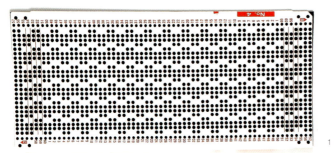

6

1 Punch cards and plastic clips for making patterned knits. Pre-punched patterns are available, which can be used with other stitch settings such as lace, tuck and slip.

2 Machine needles feature a latch, a hook and butt. There are more needles to a fine gauge machine and fewer needles to a chunky gauge machine.

3 Latch tools are used for casting off and picking up dropped stitches.

4 Transfer tools for moving stitches from one needle to another. Two- and three-prong tools are useful for handling two groups of stitches simultaneously, such as cables. Adjustable pronged tools enable you to set some prongs in non-working positions; these can be as big as 15 prongs to a tool.

5 Repair tools are useful for picking up dropped stitches. These come in a variety of styles and tend to look like crochet hooks; some have double-ended combinations of pick (pointed) and transfer (eyelet).

6 Hole punch for making punch cards.

7 Plastic needle pushers. To speed up the needle selection, these enable you to select a number of needles at once, depending on the arrangement of their teeth; for example, you can push or pull every second, third or fourth needle.

8 Mylar sheet for making patterned knits on an electronic machine. No hole punch is required as patterns are drawn on to the sheet with a soft pencil that reflects the light.

7

8

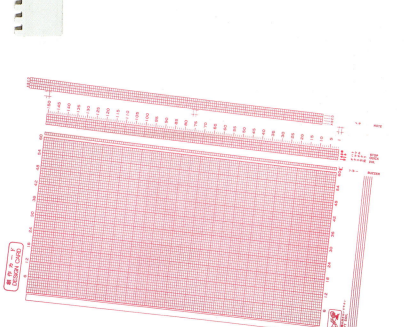

9 Winders are useful for winding yarn on to cones or into balls. Variations of these are available, which are used for twisting yarns together.

10 Ribber combs and weights, supplied with the ribber, are used for casting on. The weights can be added to the comb as needed.

11 Open-hooked combs are used for single bed casting on and as additional weights with larger pieces of knit.

12 Wire-edge hangers are useful tools for weighting small groups of stitches on double bed knitting. They are handy for edges to prevent unwanted loops at the end of rows.

13 Claw weights help keep stitches firmly in place on the needles. These can be moved easily as the knitting grows. They come in a variety of shapes and sizes; some weights have holes, allowing additional weights to be hung from them.

14 Nylon cord is useful for casting on when an unfinished edge of knitting is required.

9

10

11

15   Industrial machine weights are suspended from either end of the comb. These are circular and can be mounted on top of each other. The amount of weight depends principally on the width of the knitting: less weight is used for fine, delicate materials.

Not pictured:
Garter bar for turning knitting over to produce a garter stitch. Ridges of reversed knit can be made.

Stitch holders. Some hand-manipulated techniques require stitches to be temporarily moved away from the needles while other knitting continues; these stitches are placed on holding tools. A capped stitch holder is designed to hold multiple stitches and stitches can

be easily replaced. Flexible circular hand-knitting needles also make useful stitch holders, as do large safety pins.

Linkers for sewing seams or attaching edges, frills and collars. They can be used to produce an edge-to-edge finish; available as hand and motorised models and also as machine accessories.

12   13

10

13

14

15

Developments in design and technology

1   Issey Miyake was the inspiration
     for this CAD knit development by
     Amy Dyer.
2   Some of the latest knitwear and yarn
     technology is displayed at Pitti Filati.
     This trade fair is the main international
     event for the knitting yarn industry.

Knitting machines have come a long way since William Lee's knitting frame in 1589. Today's streamlined systems and knitted fabrics have advanced in design and quality as a result of evolving technologies in computers and yarn manufacture.

As we have discovered, hand-knitted seamless garments date back to medieval times and the fisherman's gansey was a highly technical, seamless garment; however, it was the introduction of the Shima Seiki machine in the 1970s that brought the concept of seamless (whole) garments to the industry. By the 1980s Shima Seiki had computerised its machines.

Another important development in knitwear manufacturing was the Japanese designer Issey Miyake's A-poc clothing concept in the 1990s. A-poc (which literally means a piece of cloth) is warp-knitted and uses a different technology to the weft-knitted, whole garment

1

concept of Shima Seiki. A-poc consists of a knitted tubular roll of cloth, which incorporates the outlines of garment shapes. Cutting lines are provided within the pattern of the knit and the customer can cut through the patterned shapes releasing a collection of garments from the same piece of cloth. This revolutionary clothing requires no seaming or finishing processes: because of the warp knit structure, the cut edges do not unravel.

There are many contrasts within knitwear design and production and, although design and developments are indeed linked to technological advancements, luxury fashion garments have always been associated with the handmade. New, innovative designs are being merged with old, traditional techniques. In response to the success of mass production there has been an increasing appreciation of 'slow clothes' and desirable, one-off garments that are more personal to the wearer.

2

'Design development allows you to make mistakes; without screwing up once in a while you can't ever move forward.'

Alexander McQueen

1   Knitwear by Cooperative Designs, A/W09. Formed by designers Annalisa Dunn and Dorothee Hagemann, Cooperative Designs is a knitwear label with an avant-garde approach.

As a knitwear student you will be expected to work independently from set project briefs. You will develop concept ideas through the use of personal research, the exploration of technical skills and design development. A good body of work and a series of design outcomes should be produced for assessment. The brief outlines the aims and learning outcomes for the project. It details the work required and explains the assessment method and criteria. Projects have to be completed within a timescale and these deadlines are important for assessment.

Research projects are usually given to students to complete over the summer break, which allows them to draw from different sources and gather a good variety of inspiration for development in the new term. Sometimes projects are linked together in order to push research and design development in different directions for separate outcomes, such as textiles for fashion or interiors.

This chapter guides you through the design process, from a knitwear project brief through to research and analysis skills and design development. You will need to have market awareness, as well as technical ability and good presentation skills, in order to achieve design realisation.

Approach to knit > **Creative development >** Construction through pattern and texture

1

The brief

1   Body of research by Karli
    Broadbent, taking inspiration
    from architecture and the urban
    landscape.

At college or university you will respond to briefs that are written and set by tutors. In your final year, however, you will be working towards your final degree collection and you will be expected to set your own project brief. Occasionally, competition briefs are set by companies within the industry, which offer a valuable insight into the commercial world. The aims of these projects are specific to the company brand and consumer market, making the costs and price range of design an important, additional, factor. Those students who successfully meet these briefs can win sponsorship, placement awards and travel bursaries.

Examine the following exercise, based on a brief that was given to year-one knitwear students at Northbrook College, in the UK.

Design workshop: surface design

Select one of the following themes to produce a collection of six to eight swatches. The swatches should be approximately 30 x 40cm (12 x 16in). Direct your designs towards fashion or interiors, showing an indication of end use, with shaped swatches and design illustrations. Your final collection should be supported by a sketchbook filled with drawings, textural developments, magazine tears and developmental trials on the knitting machine.
Two mood boards, approximately 30 x 58cm (16 x 23in) are required, explaining colour mood and theme. You will also need to carry out a comparative survey of current knitted trends. This will involve a brief written analysis (250 words) of new trends in knitted fabrics at one chain store, one department store and one brand-led retailer.

Themes

Texture
Look at edges; extremes of surfaces; hairy and smooth; shiny and matt; yarns with texture, such as mohair, bouclé, rayon and lambswool; look to the environment for inspiration.

Embellishment
Include embroidery, beading, sequins, florals, lace, geometrics, appliqué, over-printing and foiling. Look at vintage pieces for inspiration.

Properties of stripe
Variation of scale, repeat, engineered designs, diagonals, flashes of colour, trimmings and multiples. Look at shirting fabrics, herringbones. Take inspiration from urban environments.

Project aims

To familiarise students with knitting machines.
To encourage use of experimentation using a
broad range of media and techniques.
To produce an imaginative and exciting range of
design ideas.
To develop processes and issues associated with
design development.
To develop a professional range of fashion
swatches.
To demonstrate market awareness.
To thoroughly research a given theme.
To encourage development of creative project
presentation.
To develop the concept of self-evaluation.

Learning outcomes and work required

The learning outcomes enable the student
to demonstrate a development in technical
knowledge and skills in knitted textiles and the
ability to produce self-initiated research. The
criteria used to assess the work include research
analysis, creative development, technical skills,
market awareness, design realisation, self
management, presentation and evaluation. The
work required for assessment is as follows:

One sketchbook filled with textural developments,
imaginative research exploring a variety of media
and colour development.
6–8 knitted swatches.
Fashion drawings (or interior room plan).
Two mood boards explaining colour, mood and
theme.
250-word market research analysis.
Self-evaluation.
Updated technical file.

Research

1–2   Sketchbooks by Cathrin
      Evans, illustrating the sources
      of inspiration and the design
      development process.

Designers are constantly seeking and collecting new ideas and sources of inspiration. Good designers need enquiring minds in order to continually produce fresh, contemporary work. A sketchbook is, in many ways, a visual diary. It offers an insight into the designer's personal creative journey. Designers develop an identity through the way they collect and process research; this is a skill that should become second nature over time. Many interesting starting points for design can be found through the ongoing investigation and individual approach to a concept or theme. Every newly found piece of knowledge feeds the imagination and brings up new questions and pathways to follow.

Specialist libraries are great starting points for research. Colleges and universities will have libraries that cater for fashion and textile courses, offering a variety of costume history, craft technique, fashion and textile books. Look out too, for intriguing out-of-print books, new and vintage magazines and newspaper clippings. The internet is also a huge resource for research and images. Some designers arrange their inspiration and research ideas on a wall, assembling visual pathways through interesting connections and the juxtaposition of images, fabric samples and sketches. Other designers develop research books and sketchbooks that reflect the thought process behind the project from start to finish. However a designer chooses to work, the ingredients remain the same: all research should include silhouettes, colours, textures, patterns, fabrics, trimmings and yarns, as well as found objects, photos, sketches and notes. Research becomes more personal when it is manipulated in some way; working into an image with collage, pen or ink can make the inspiration unique.

Primary sources

Drawing from a primary source will help you to understand details of shape and form. It is important that you seek original sources to draw from in order to record the image in a personal way. Drawing is a valuable tool; it not only allows you to communicate ideas to others but it can be used to record personal choices. Smaller elements of the image can be examined; parts of an image can be enlarged or repeated. Drawing helps to record and document the process of development. Take photographs, make sketches and highlight elements through the use of paint, crayon, ink or collage.

Market research

Market research involves collecting a range of visual trend information, which should be used to inform and inspire your work, while reflecting the season and target market. You need to know who the consumers of your designs are; where they will be found; how many there are and whether or not it is a growing market. You should also research the kind of price they would be prepared to pay for a product; whether they have a preference for one brand above another and, if so, what and why. It is also worth considering furnishings and fashion accessories when assessing the market.

Design workshop

Produce a written analysis of new trends in knitted fabrics. Visit a number of different retail outlets, such as chain stores, department stores and brand-led retailers:

1   Consider the store layout – what is the overall feel?
2   Is there a strong colour mood? Does the mood occur in all stores?
3   What is the quality of the knit? What is the finish?
4   Are there any strong embellishment trends, such as beading?
5   Do the goods look like they are value for money; what is the price point?

Concepts and themes

A designer will often focus on a particular concept or theme to enable the design process and give focus to a project. A narrative theme forms the basis of many collections; a theme that will convey a mood and tell a story. The designer will often use a subject of personal interest, one that can stimulate ideas and help to give a visual impact to a final collection.

A concept or theme helps to hold the work together, giving it continuity and coherence. A good example of a strong narrative theme is Alexander McQueen's Autumn/Winter 2001 'What a Merry-Go-Round' collection. The show opened in darkness, which emphasised the circular lighting from a full-size merry-go-round. The collection was a mixture of military-inspired suits and coats with sashes and braids, tall hats with plumes, showgirls' headdresses combined with helmets and heavy, black knitted sweaters featuring images of skeletons. The chilling music added suspense and, as the music changed, the merry-go-round began to slowly turn. This collection was dedicated to the people of change and revolution.

Another way of processing your work is through the use of an abstract concept, such as the connotation of a single word. Words such as cocoon, wrap or layer can be used to sustain a whole project and trigger interesting starting points for development. Designer Shelley Fox is known for her abstract concepts and thought-provoking collections. For her Autumn/Winter 2001 collection she used her diaries as inspiration. The diary print was taken from a series of Shelley Fox business diaries; certain pages were selected based on their composition and assembled to make a print. The collection was a mixture of evening sweat shirting, cashmere, diary scribble graphic prints and oversized cable knitwear.

The colours were a natural palette of black, putty and highlights of mint green, bright reds and primrose yellows. For her Autumn/Winter 1998 collection she used the concept of Braille, which inspired a development into the use of Braille markings on wool (felted knit). This fabric was then transformed into three-dimensional geometric shapes, which were drafted on the body.

1   Grey wool felt Braille top by Shelley Fox, A/W98.

2   Knitwear from the A/W01 'What a Merry Go Round' collection by Alexander McQueen.

3   Diary print skirt by Shelley Fox, A/W01.

1

Project work can also be developed from a combination of unrelated images or a contrast of ideas such as 'natural/man-made', 'urban/orchard' or 'food/fiction'. The quality of your final outcomes will be determined by the breadth, quality and individuality of your initial and on-going research. Costume houses, museums, exhibitions, markets and antique fairs, charity shops and holidays abroad can all provide great sources of inspiration. You need to be able to fully explore the concept in order to create a collection of experimental and innovative knitted samples, which in turn will inspire ideas for a final fashion collection.

2

3

The brief > **Research** > Design development

Design development

1–2 Presentation boards by Amy Dyer, showing the design development and how the inspiration sources have been translated into pattern design and knitted samples.

Your research drawings will be developed into design ideas for patterns and textures. These ideas should then inspire your knitted fabrics and fashion collections. Put together mood boards from selected elements of your research, to help you organise your thoughts and collate ideas. Mood boards are an essential tool in industry for selling projects and gaining commissions. A mood board is a way for you to visually introduce your project; it should demonstrate to your client the theme, colour and feel of a project without your having to be there to elaborate, and it should be visually stimulating. Be very selective about the images you pick to use on your board – every photo, picture and fabric should be perfect; if it isn't, you should make it so. Try to include original art. If using found images, such as other people's photos and magazine tears, then manipulate them – change the colour, paint over them, layer and distort them. As a general rule, less is more, so try not to clutter your board. There are no rules on layout for mood boards, but they tend to look better with a plain border.

Begin to explore a variety of creative possibilities by translating your research images into knitted sample trials. For example, a piece of woven fabric could be the inspiration for a pattern; a plastic tablecloth might inspire a knitted lace. Make the project as personal as possible. Using your research, you will be expected to construct and experiment using a variety of techniques. Along with traditional drawing styles and experimental mark making, consider paper/fabric manipulations; collect and create a variety of textures through machine stitching, cut work, layering and folding. Work in both two-dimensional and three-dimensional ways to produce different design outcomes. Consider silhouette and try playing with scale: for example, a folded doily could inspire the shape of a sleeve. Review and evaluate your research work, extract the most successful outcomes and develop these further into a range of knitted samples.

1

2

Knitted samples

The next stage is to begin sampling, using a combination of coloured and textured yarns with stitch construction to take your research forward into fabrics. Use your mood boards and research to extract textures, patterns and silhouettes. A paper-cut experiment might now become the template for a knitted punch card pattern. A stitched fabric experiment could inform a knitted stripe or weave. A drawing of an air vent in the Metro can become the start of a knitted transfer or partial knit lace pattern. In order to create a range of interesting samples, you will need to gather a good mixture of yarns in different colours, textures and thicknesses. Experiment with knitting one stitch construction or pattern at a time, using a variety of different yarns and tensions. Try mixtures of yarns, in stripes or blocks of colour; or contrasting textures, such as thick yarn with thin; translucent with matt, shiny or both. Spend time sampling, sorting and trying out ideas; it is not just about simply knitting different colourways.

When you have a good idea of which yarns work well with which techniques, you can begin to explore a mixture of stitch constructions. You might want to mix lace holes with partial knit or tuck stitch with a weave or add a partial stripe. The tension on the machine will need to be changed in order to accommodate different yarns; this takes patience, and a lot of practice, in the beginning.

When you have explored all the options, you will need to decide which ideas to develop further into your final outcomes. As you edit and prioritise a selection from your first samples, you may find that a number of samples already sit well together as a collection and translate well into garment ideas. Any developments of first samples that will be used for your final collections should be added to your research book as you go. Although knitwear is versatile, keep in mind the quality of the fabrics when designing your fashion collection. Soft, draping fabrics, for example, are suitable for dresses; thicker, heavier

weights can be used for jackets. Above all, the fabrics and designs should capture the mood of the project. Your collection should reflect the customer and market and suit the season for which it is intended.

1

Design workshop

Knitted samples should be approximately 50 stitches wide and 10cm (4in) long. Consider the following:

1 Pick a stitch construction, such as tuck, weave, Fair Isle, transfer lace or partial knit.
2 Play with extremes of tension.
3 Use different colours. Try different textures.
4 Explore a combination of stitch constructions.

Build up a technical file, containing notes of the different tensions, yarns and techniques. First samples should also be kept in the technical file as a useful source of reference.

1–3   A selection of knitted samples by Sarah Nicholls (1) and Ruth Carpenter (2–3). These examples clearly illustrate how the designers have used their research to develop textures and patterns.

2

3

Colour

1–4 Series of sketchbook pages by
Lucy Faulke (1–2) and Ruth Carpenter
(3–4), which show the development
of colour combinations using yarn
samples and paint.

At the beginning of a project you should establish a colour mood and create a colour mood board. To allow for some adjustments, it is a good idea to have a working board at the beginning and a final finished board towards the end of the project. Colours are essential tools for anyone working in the fashion industry. You will need to develop a good colour sense and be aware of colour trends.

Sampling and swatch making is a great way of developing colour awareness. It gives you the opportunity to learn about colour in relation to proportion and to gain an understanding of how colours react when placed next to each other. Try out colour combinations for stripes by winding differently coloured yarns around narrow pieces of card. This will enable you to see the overall final look at a glance; it not only helps you to decide the width of stripe, but also the number of colours to use in a repeat pattern. Similar effects can be achieved with paint and with different widths of cut or stitched strips of coloured paper laid next to each other.

Views on the use of colour and pattern will vary from person to person but most people agree that certain colours have common associations. We tend to associate some colours with urban life and others with rural; some we think of as warm colours, others as cool. These assumptions will affect our response to the work, just as likes and dislikes of colours can make or break a design. Many historical pieces of knit are appealing because of the complicated hand techniques, but colour is just as important: the colours of a Fair Isle knit, for example, must be a visually appealing combination. There are many ways to combine colour: you may prefer colours with a lived-in quality about them, such as muted tones of black to grey and shades of brown to beige; or you may prefer strong, vivid colours with patterns to emphasise harsh contrasts. Sometimes it is valuable to challenge your preferences. Try to move outside your comfort zone by choosing to work with colour ranges you do not personally prefer.

1

2

3

4

1–2 Colour trend
information
is displayed
at trade fairs
such as Pitti
Filati (1) and
Première
Vision (2).

1

2

Colour trend forecasting

There are many colour trend forecast companies that predict colours every season for different aspects of the fashion industry, such as lingerie, leather, shoes, accessories and so on. Designers and product buyers are also often responsible for predicting colour choices. Larger companies employ teams of people to produce colour mood prediction boards. The process of colour trend forecasting involves predicting groups of colours and dividing them into themed categories, with colour and mood descriptions for promotion. Fibre and yarn manufacturers purchase colour forecasting information to assist them in the making of their shade cards, which in turn also serve as prediction packages. Fabric and knitwear manufacturers then choose their colours from both the

colour forecasting companies and the fibre and yarn shade cards. This information is usually available at trade exhibitions, such as Pitti Filati in Florence and Première Vision in Paris.

The consumer may be influenced by colour trends advertised in magazines but in the end, colour predictions are only effective if the consumer buys the product.

Try mixing unusual colour combinations. Look at art, fabric, wallpaper samples and gift wrap. Work out the colour combinations used and decide if you think the combinations work or not, and why.

Experiment with contrasting pairs; these can be subtle or dramatic. Create combinations using three, four, five and six colours.

Try combinations of similar tones and shades. You could try several shades of one colour and then add a single row of contrast.

Explore patterns in neutral colours, whites, off-whites, beiges and greys.

Produce a colour concept; for example, you could try combining delicate old rose, gold and ivory for a vintage palette.

Sculptural form

A three-dimensional approach to your work considers shape and form, proportion, volume and weight. It takes your fabric design into garment ideas. This is an extremely important research and design process and should be documented in sketchbooks throughout the project with the use of notes, sketches and photographs.

Using your research, start to translate shapes into quarter-scale or part-garment ideas and manipulate dress pattern pieces to inspire shapes for possible sleeves, collars and so on. Many ideas for shape and structure can be tried out with a mannequin, some stretch jersey toile fabric and knitted trial samples, pattern cutting paper and a box of pins. As a designer, you will need to understand the behaviour of knitted fabric on the body, so experiment with various stretch jersey fabrics in order to find a similar weight to the final knit. Shape making and fabric development should happen simultaneously; each one affects the other. If your starting point is a range of knitted swatches, already produced, then the construction of your garments will be determined by the weight and structure of your knit.

Colour > **Sculptural form** > Presentation and evaluation

Design process

1–3 Series of pages from portfolio by Lucy Faulke, showing the development of sculptural designs on the stand.

You can incorporate interesting structural aspects of your knitting techniques to direct design ideas. For example, a knitted piece that has a placement of increased elasticity may be used where it could help the design, such as in the waist or the small of the back. Knitting techniques and pattern placement should work for you, to help the fit of the garment. Large knitted samples can be wrapped around the mannequin to create sections of garments; this method of creating shape is particularly effective when the fabric features a partial knit technique. Many unexpected folds and drapes can be achieved through an asymmetric wrap and drape. The missing parts of the garment can then be filled in with jersey toile fabric and turned into patterns, which in turn will be knitted. Each stage provides important information for you to develop into your designs.

Look at how the fabric behaves when it is shaped on the body and design your pieces accordingly. You will achieve the best results when you become totally engaged in the process, continually working between 3D modelling on the mannequin and sampling on the machine; trying out elements of fit and drape, altering and correcting pieces, to realise the desired size, scale, weight or shape.

1

2

3

Creating volume

1   Sculptural collar by Juliana Sissons.
Photography by Mitchell Sams.

2   Portfolio by Victoria Hill, showing the
development of sculptural designs on
the stand.

All knit can be moulded around the body but consider the weight of the fabric when creating volume. Lightweight jerseys can drape into soft folds but bulky knitted fabric can be solid and heavy.

Large structures can be quickly built with thick yarns and large needles on a chunky gauge machine. Volume and shape can also be achieved through the use of repetition: layer upon layer of fine knit can be used to create large silhouettes of light, feathery bulk. Draping, frills and pleating techniques are other ways to add volume and shape to lightweight knits.

Designing garments and making patterns come about through a combination of procedures and starting points. You may prefer, as a sculptor does, to start with an illustration of a garment or a sketch of an idea, or to work directly on a mannequin with a stretch jersey fabric, modelling and pinning together various sections to achieve the desired effect and silhouette. This method offers a more immediate look at the proportions and design details of a garment (you can pencil on to the toile any alterations of seam lines, placement of pockets, neck openings and so on) before starting to develop the weight and drape of the knit.

My idea: by slicing up an area of the painting into a section
it created an interesting shape as seen on the right ⟶
The shape looks quite aggressive, sharp, fierce and edgy which
is similar to the characteristics of the 'personality' Peggy
I placed the pattern pieces that I printed out over the body
which is shown in the pictures on the following pages.
The idea would be to develop it into a jacket made
out of laser cut leather / high quality breatllled felted fabric.

FRONT   BACK   Left side   Right side

2

Presentation and evaluation

1   Swatch by Annabel Scopes, designed
    on an electronic machine with the
    DesignaKnit package.
2   Swatch by Annabel Scopes, made
    on a chunky gauge Dubied machine.
    Needles from the front bed have been
    transferred to the back bed to create
    the pattern.

At the end of a project, you will be expected to display and present your work for a group discussion and evaluation. This will provide the opportunity to develop presentation skills, engage in critical self-reflection, comment on and learn from the work of your peers, share experiences, receive constructive criticism (and offer it to others) and develop the ability to articulate your design intentions. A written self-evaluation offers you a chance to write down your thoughts on the project process (your performance and development) and your work.

Display of samples and swatches

Knitted swatches can be attached to display headers, which are narrow pieces of card that fold over the top of the swatch, allowing the fabric to hang free. Swatches can also be mounted on display sheets, made from mid-weight card or mount board. Swatches can be kept separate from the design illustrations, but in many cases finished illustrations are drawn on to these boards, showing final design ideas.

Knitted sample trials can be mounted on design development boards, which act as visual extensions to your sketch books. A design development board should document the different stages of work, including sketches, diagrams and photos of your three-dimensional work, to illustrate your process whilst allowing interaction with your design vision.

Choose the best samples for presentation; any additional samples can be put in your technical file or sketchbook. A selection of knitted samples looks good attached to your mood boards, as both theme and colour can be communicated through intensity of stitch. For example, a closely knitted thick yarn, with vivid blocks of colour, would suggest a different mood and colour theme to an open lace knit of fine yarn in delicate pastel shades.

Remember not to stick swatches down on all sides – the knit needs to be handled for evaluation.

Fashion drawings

You need to be able to communicate your design ideas effectively, choosing the most appropriate illustration style for your work. Front and back views are often necessary to get a complete picture. Your design illustrations, which will be added to presentation boards, need to be clear but also convey texture and design detail. Inspirational material may often be included on a presentation board, which serves to reinforce the mood of the collection. Scale and proportion is important: the illustrations should represent correct sizing and the silhouette should be accurate.

Flat working drawings can be added to the presentation board alongside more creative illustrations. These flat drawings are usually referred to as specification or technical drawings and are used in the fashion industry to communicate to the pattern cutter, machinist or knitter. These drawings accurately describe how garments are constructed, showing precise proportions, measurements, positioning of seams, pockets, fastenings and neckline details. These technical or working drawings should also be kept in your technical file, along with measurements, yarn details, costs, sample swatches and pattern instructions.

2

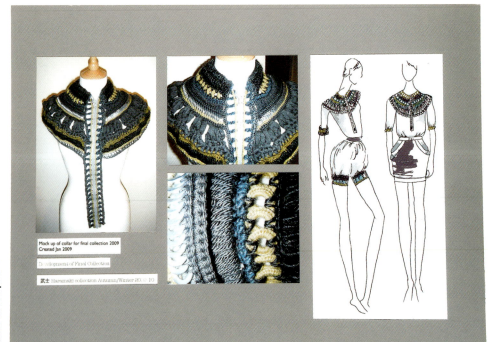

Mock up of collar for final collection 2009
Created Jan 2009

Development of Final Collection

武士 Haramaki collection Autumn/Winter 20__10

Self-evaluation

The purpose of self-evaluation is to learn from experience. This will help you to adapt, modify and develop strategies for future action, in order to improve your working methods and design outcomes. If you evaluate and plan in this manner, it will not only improve your overall performance, but you will also become more independent and begin to take responsibility for your own learning.

Your sketchbook is a good place to start. Sketchbooks that have been developed throughout the project should provide a reflective commentary alongside the design work. One page should relate to another, telling a story and documenting your exploration. It should be a highly personal piece of work, individual to you, your inspirations and methods of working.

Each stage of research and design development is important, from two-dimensional drawings and patterns to three-dimensional textiles; from the knitted sample trials to the finished shaped swatches. The combination of these different elements will give you clearer focus on the design concept, helping you to form a good working method and a format that can be developed for all conceptual projects.

As you continue on your course, you will be expected to show increasing self-awareness and to develop an understanding of your work and working methods. You will be expected to direct your own progress and to identify your strengths and areas to develop.

Design workshop

At the end of a project, ask yourself the following questions:
Did your research inspire you?
Did you have enough primary research?
Did you explore the most interesting parts of your research?
Did you exhaust each creative pathway and make the most of your ideas?
Were you happy with your colourways?
Were you inspired by your choice of yarns?
Did you push the processes and techniques chosen and explore new ground?
Were your final fabric swatches suitable for your design ideas?
Did your fashion collection represent the season specified?
Did the collection fit the target market?
What did you learn?
What would you have done differently?
What will you do next?
What ideas have you now developed, which you would like to push further?

1–2   Presentation boards by Lucy Faulke, showing final designs, drawings and design development.

Sculptural form > **Presentation and evaluation**

1   Surface design on lace by Katie
     Laura White.

*'The essence and beauty of knit lies in the fact that the
designer invents everything from scratch; he creates the
stitch, the handle, the weight and chooses the colour,
deciding on texture and shape at the same time,
mastering his own finishings and detailing.'*

Li Edelkoort

Three-dimensional effects in surface texture can be created
through a combination of knit stitch techniques and different
weight yarns. Once you have mastered basic stitch variations
and pattern techniques you can really begin to experiment
with knit. In chapter 3 we look at the use of pattern and texture
in construction, with basic knitting techniques on domestic
machines. There are exercises in stripes and tension
changes, patterns, modern lace and textural effects,
such as cables and weave.

It is important to keep a technical file, which will be of constant
aid throughout your studies. Collate and record all your knitted
tension swatches, along with notes of the fabric qualities and
suitability for design. You should be able to use your technical
file to reproduce samples if necessary. The file will be an
ongoing personal resource and you should keep adding
to it for every project.

1

The tension swatch

1 Knitted tension swatches featuring ladders and open spaces.
2 Knitting a tension swatch enables you to calculate the number of rows between different colours, as shown here.
3 These swatches feature a combination of rib and different size stitches.

It is very important to achieve the correct tension when knitting a garment. A tension swatch is vital for knitting a garment to the correct size and fabric quality; it enables you to calculate how many stitches to cast on, how many rows to knit and how many needles are needed to increase or decrease during shaping. If your garment involves lacework or changes of technique within the fabric, these details will need to be knitted into the tension swatch; quite often, many tension swatches are knitted for one garment.

When using an existing knitting pattern, the tension measurement will be provided with the pattern instruction. A set of measurements such as 30 stitches and 40 rows to 10cm (4in), for example, means that you will need to cast on 30 needles and knit 40 rows to achieve a 10cm (4in) square. If you do not match the tension measurement with a correct tension swatch, your work may not fit correctly and you will need to vary the tension settings. It is important to keep a record of these tension swatches, alongside yarn and machine gauge details, in your technical file for future reference.

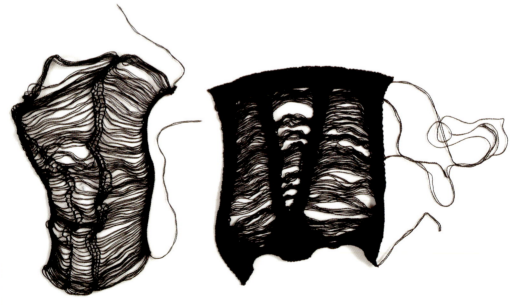

2

3

Making tension swatches

There are various ways of making tension swatches and most knitters find a way that best suits their needs. Here are two of the most common ways: measuring tension and calculating a tension square.

Note: the measurements here are in metric. To convert to imperial, 1cm = 2/5in.

Calculating rows per centimetre
50 rows = 13.5cm
100 rows = 27cm
100/27 = 3.7
3.7 rows = 1cm

Calculating stitches per centimetre
50 stitches = 15cm
100 stitches = 30cm
100/30 = 3.3
3.3 stitches = 1cm

Measuring tension

1   Knit a swatch that is approximately 80 needles wide and approximately 20cm long, using the yarn you have selected for the garment. Make a note of how many rows you have knitted. (Note: if you are matching a set of tension measurements, you will need to cast on a further 20 or so needles and knit approximately 30 more rows, so that the swatch is wider and longer than the tension measurements provided; this is because the edge stitches can be distorted.)
2   Take the swatch off the machine, wash or steam it and place it on a flat surface. Finish it in the same way you will finish your final garments.
3   Choose an area on the sample where the knitting looks fairly even; not close to an edge where it may be distorted.
4   Measure 10cm widthways and mark the stitches with pins. Count the number of stitches between the pins. To calculate the number of stitches per centimetre, divide the total by 10.
5   Measure 10cm lengthways and mark the rows with pins. Count the number of rows between the pins. To calculate the numbers of rows per centimetre, divide the total by 10.
6   Note the gauge of the machine, along with the type, thickness, colour and brand of yarn (it is good practice to write this on a label and attach it to the swatch). This will enable you to match tension swatches at a later stage.

Many knitted samples from your trials could also work as tension swatches for patterns in different textures. But remember, when matching your tension swatch to tension measurements provided (such as 30 stitches and 40 rows to 10cm), the measurements must be correct. If the 30 stitches measure less than 10cm, then the knitting is too tight and will need to be knitted again on a looser tension or on a larger gauge machine. If the 30 stitches measure more than 10cm, the knitting is too loose and will need to be knitted on a tighter tension or a finer gauge machine. Similarly, if the 40 rows measure more or less than 10cm, then the tension will need to be adjusted accordingly.

1   Tension swatches by Annabel Scopes
     showing a combination of stitch
     techniques.

Calculating a tension square

Another way of tension swatching is to measure from a square of 50 needles and 50 rows to calculate the amount of stitches and rows per centimetre. This information is used when drafting knitting patterns.

1   Thread the machine with waste yarn; this can be the same type or weight as the yarn intended for the garment, but in a contrasting colour.
2   Cast on approximately 80 needles. This allows the finished width to be wider than the 50 needles needed, thus avoiding any distorted edge stitches.
3   Knit 15 or 20 rows in waste yarn.
4   Change to the same yarn that you will be using for the garment. Knit 50 rows. It is a good idea to pause at 25 rows and put markers in the middle of the swatch to indicate where the 50 stitches are. Markers can be made by hooking a contrast colour yarn on to needles 1 and 50.
5   Change back to waste yarn and knit 15 or 20 rows before binding off.
6   Wash or steam the tension swatch and allow the knit to settle.
7   Place your tension swatch on a flat surface, ready for measuring and calculation. If, for example, 50 rows measures 13.5cm, we can assume that 100 rows would measure 27cm. To calculate the number of rows in 1 centimetre, we divide 100 by 27, which equals 3.7 rows per centimetre. Then, if 50 stitches measures 15cm, we can assume 100 stitches would measure 30cm. To calculate the number of stitches in 1 centimetre, we divide 100 by 30, giving 3.3 stitches per centimetre.

Note: as it is not possible to knit 3.7 rows or 3.3 stitches, the final measurement should be rounded up or down.

Basic techniques

There are a number of basic techniques that you will need to learn as a beginner. Casting on, binding off and picking up dropped stitches are all hand-manipulated effects that appear in one way or another; they can also be used in combination with other techniques for interesting results. It is a good idea to spend some time practising these fundamental skills so that you can confidently use them in your knitting.

There are many ways of casting on and binding off, each of which creates individual edges and visual finish detail. Casting-on and binding-off techniques are not only used at the beginning and end of a knit, they are also used for shaping, lace techniques and buttonholes.

Closed edge cast-on

1 Thread the yarn through the tension spring and disc. Pull yarn down to the left side of the machine.
2 Move the required number of needles to holding position (when the needles are pushed forward in the bed as far as they will go).
3 Make a slip knot and place on the end of the left-hand needle. With the carriage on the right, work from left to right, winding the yarn anti-clockwise (this is known as an 'e-wrap').
4 After wrapping the last needle on the right, thread the yarn into the carriage.
5 Take the carriage across to knit. Move needles out again and repeat until there are enough rows on which to hang weights. Knit the required length.

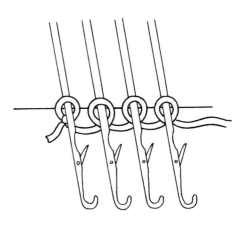

Open edge cast-on

1 Thread yarn through the tension spring, disc and carriage on the right side of the machine.
2 Move the required number of needles to working position.
3 Knit one row with waste yarn. Hold on to the end of the yarn whilst moving the carriage across the needles. This will look like a row of loops.
4 Place a length of nylon cord across the loops, between the needles and the sinker gate pegs (the row of pegs along the front of the needle bed). Holding both ends of the cord firmly in one hand, pull down.
5 Keeping the cord firmly in place, knit 10 rows or until the knit is long enough to hang weights on.
6 Remove the cord, gently pulling at one end. Continue knitting or change to intended yarn.

Casting on

Two useful casting-on techniques include the 'closed edge cast-on' by hand, which will not unravel as it creates a firm, solid edge; and the 'open edge cast-on,' which produces an open edge of loops that can either be knitted on to at a later time, or turned up to make a hem.

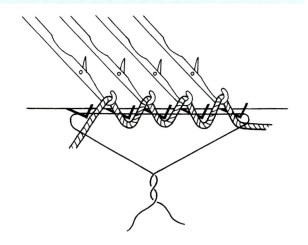

Needle positions

There are four needle positions on most domestic knitting machines (although the Passap has two). On either end of the needle bed you will find a set of engraved letters: A, B, C and D on a Knitmaster; A, B, D and E on a Brother. To operate the needles, you will need to align their butts with the letters. The positions are as follows:

- A: needles are in non-working position and do not knit (NWP)
- B: needles are in working position (WP)
- C (D for Brother): needles are in upper working position (UWP)
- D (E for Brother): needles are in holding position (HP) and do not knit when holding cam levers are on.

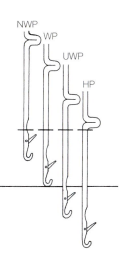

NWP
WP
UWP
HP

The tension swatch > Basic techniques > Lace

Binding off (casting off)

When finishing a piece of knitting, all stitches should be secured with a firm, neat edge. As with casting on, there are various ways of binding off. The following method requires the use of a transfer tool. It may be easier to remove the yarn from the carriage and tension unit but, if not, pull enough yarn down through the feeder to take away the tension. Always cast off from the same side as the carriage.

Cast-off technique

1   Place the transfer tool on to the first needle. Pull out and push back so that the stitch moves on to the transfer tool.
2   Place the stitch onto the next needle (either behind or in front of the sinker gate pegs). Pull this needle out so that the two stitches fall behind the needle latch.
3   Take the yarn from the feeder and lie it across the needle hook, but in front of the latch. Pull the needle back to knit a new stitch. Two stitches have been knitted into one and one stitch has been cast off.
4   Repeat this process until the end of the knitting. Cast off the last stitch by pulling the end of the cut yarn through the stitch.

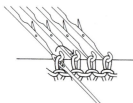

1

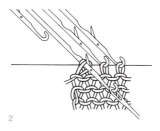

2

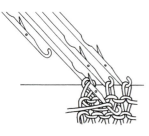

3

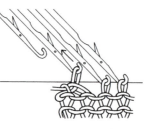

4

Reforming stitches

To repair a dropped stitch you need to use a latch tool to reform the stitch by hand. If a stitch has dropped through several rows it can be picked up and re-knitted.

Reforming a dropped stitch

1   Insert a latch tool from behind the knitting, directly into the stitch below the one that needs reforming.
2   Push the latch tool forward, allowing the stitch to fall behind the latch. Catch the next floating thread in the hook and pull the latch tool back, closing the latch with the thread inside.
3   Pull the latch tool further back, so that the stitch slides down over the closed latch, forming a new stitch in the hook.
4   Continue to pick up any more floats, always taking the one directly above the stitch.
5   When reaching the top, use a single transfer tool to place the stitch back on to the needle (see illustration below).

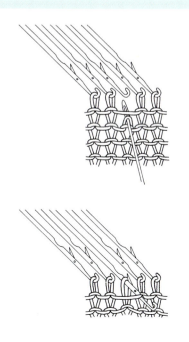

Technical file

Once you have mastered the basic casting-on and plain knitting techniques you will start to become familiar with the machine and its workings. Keep all your findings in your technical file. Ideally, the file should contain the following:

- How the knitting machine works, the function of the carriage, and so on.
- Care and maintenance of the machine.
- Knitted samples of manually produced patterns: tension testing, stripes, lace-holes, ladders and finishing details, such as hemming and buttonholes.
- Knitted samples of punch-card or Mylar sheet patterns, such as Fair Isle or slip-and-tuck stitch.
- Knitted samples of ribbed fabrics, such as different-size ribs made on the double bed machine and mock ribs made on the single bed machine.
- Design-related patterns and samples; for example, part garment ideas, such as a cuff or a collar.
- Illustrations and diagrams related to samples.
- Graph patterns used for Fair Isle designs or stitch construction.
- Notes and knitting patterns for making garments, such as fully fashioned shaping.
- CAD information and any related work, such as pattern printouts, samples and notes.
- Samples of yarn – write to manufacturers for shade cards.
- Keep cuttings of the latest knitwear trends in magazines and newspapers.

Stitch dial: tension stripes

Always ensure that the correct stitch dial number is selected for the yarn being used. The stitch dial regulates the size of the stitch. Setting the stitch dial to 0 creates the tightest (smallest) stitch. Setting the stitch dial to 10 creates the loosest (largest) stitch. If the tension is too tight it will be difficult to knit and the garment will be hard and uncomfortable to wear. If the tension is too loose, your garment will have no shape.

Practise knitting with a variety of yarns on different tensions. Lower numbers on the stitch dial are generally better for use with fine yarns and higher numbers are best suited to the thicker yarns.

After you have become accustomed to creating the correct weight and handle in your knitted fabrics, you can experiment by creating striped samples with contrasting tensions and varying thicknesses, weight, fibre content, colour and texture.

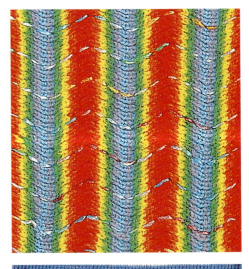

2

1

3

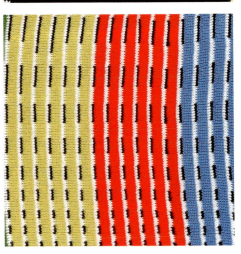

4

Construction through pattern and texture

5

6

Making stripes

1. Cast on in the normal manner and knit the required number of rows.
2. Break the yarn and thread up the second colour in the second feeder on the tension unit.
3. Pull the new and broken threads away from the direction to be knitted, to avoid loops. Knit required number of rows and repeat.
4. Try repeating numbers of rows for each colourway, then try changing numbers of rows for each colour group.

When using horizontal stripes on a garment, remember that the pieces will need to be matched up carefully when sewn together.

Vertical or diagonal stripes can be made using a punch card or Mylar sheet, by designing in CAD, or by using the partial knitting technique (holding needles).

1–8   A selection of single and double bed samples, with a mixture of plain stripe and more complex patterned stripes, by Amy Dyer, Sarah Nicholls and Natalie Osborne.

7

8

The tension swatch > **Basic techniques** > Lace

Lace

1   Lace stitch formation: a basic transfer
     stitch technique.
2   The sample chart shows an eyelet
     hole pattern for lace.
3   Lace design by knitwear designer
     Mark Fast, S/S10. Catwalking.com.

Modern lace is a combination of translucent nets and loose floats, patterned eyelets and irregular dropped stitches. It is usually knitted in lightweight, fine yarns. The use of fine yarn on a chunky gauge machine will result in a soft, transparent, pliable net. Giant stitches can be made by only casting on every second or third needle. Plain lace involves placing one stitch on to an adjacent one, to make a hole immediately next to it.

Transfer stitches

Lace knits are made using the basic transfer stitch technique, which involves transferring stitches from one set of needles to another, with the use of multi-point transfer tools. It is possible to transfer many stitches in one move. Stitches may either be transferred to other needles on the bed or allowed to drop and ladder the full length of the fabric. Automatic lace carriages are available for some single bed domestic machines. Selected stitches are transferred automatically to adjacent needles.

Several stitches can be transferred to a single needle, either to reposition stitches for patterning or to alter the shape of a ladder. A variety of eyelet designs and small buttonholes are based on the transfer stitch technique.

When working on a double bed machine, transfers can be made with a 'bodkin', a tool that has an eyelet at each end. After removing a stitch with one end of the bodkin, it can be tilted so that the stitch slides to the other end, making it easier to replace the stitch on the opposite bed.

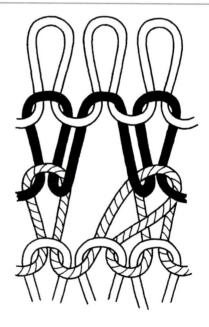

1

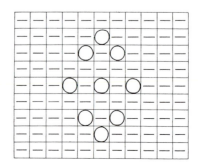

2

Lace technique / eyelet holes

1 Cast on as normal. Knit the required amount of rows.
2 Using the transfer tool, transfer one stitch to an adjacent needle and return the empty needle to position B (working position).
3 Knit two rows to close the holes.
4 More complex lace patterns can be achieved by experimenting with this basic stitch structure. Try transferring more than one stitch at a time and take them in different directions.

3

Ladders

Ladders create a lacy effect, made by an exaggerated version of the transfer stitch technique. Ladders can be made into shapes or they can be built up horizontally by transferring a stitch on one side of the ladder and putting an empty needle back into action on the other side of the ladder; this action is repeated after every row or every second row of knit.

1   Sample chart shows a ladder that is two needles wide.
2   Shaped ladder knit, with eyelet hole detail, by Juliana Sissons.
3   Lace design by Rodarte, A/W08. Catwalking.com.

1

3

Ladder technique

1   Transfer one stitch at required intervals, leaving empty needles out of action (position A). For example, you could leave every fourth needle in the non-working position. This forms a ladder whilst knitting. Bring back the empty needles to working position (position B) to continue plain knitting. This technique can be used to form decorative patterns, such as threading contrasting yarn or ribbon through the ladders.

2   Alternatively, for a ribbed effect, use a latch tool on the wrong side (purl) of the fabric and reform the stitches by picking up the floats, two at a time; continue pulling one through the other until you reach the top. This is more effective when leaving two needles out of action at regular intervals.

3   Experiment with wide ladders using multiple needles. You can create an interesting lace effect by randomly picking up floats with the latch tool and hooking them on to the nearest working needles.

4   To create a shaped ladder, try transferring stitches out from each side of the existing ladder, in between rows of knit. Leave the empty needles out of action (position A) until you reach the desired width of ladder. Then, one by one from each side, bring back the empty needles into working position (position B). Explore variations of this technique.

Note: if two adjacent needles are brought back into action at the same time, one enlarged stitch is formed, instead of two.

Surface texture

1 Knitwear collection by Tirzah Mastin, The designer created surface textures using a combination of fine and chunky yarns in silk, cotton and wool, and has incorporated devoré print, intarsia, plating and holding techniques.

Basic stitch variations will add a decorative element to your knitting and considerably change the appearance and suitability of the fabric. A fine-yarn knit, for example, can be made to look heavier by the use of fancy stitches.

The three main techniques for adding surface texture are weave, tuck stitch and slip stitch. Woven (also known as inlay) fabrics that have an all-over pattern have very little stretch widthways; these fabrics are more solid and may be cut with little damage of unravelling. Tuck stitch produces a warm bulky fabric, with lots of stretch. It is a non-curling fabric with solid edges, making it easier to make up into garments. Slip stitch creates an opaque fabric with little stretch; the all-over float patterns may be used decoratively or to create lightweight, textured fabrics with good insulating properties. Techniques such as lifting stitches and making cables are also effective ways of adding surface texture to your knit.

Tuck and slip stitches use a similar selection technique. Both types of stitch can be produced automatically, with either a punch card or Mylar sheet. Both tuck and slip stitches must be used in combination with knit stitches; each tuck needle should have a needle knitting plain either side of it. It is also possible to set the carriage to tuck or slip when moving in one direction and to plain knit in the other direction. Both tuck and slip stitches can be combined with colour striping, for colour-texture effects.

1

Lace > **Surface texture** > **Patterned knits**

Tuck stitch

Tuck stitch can produce textured pattern on both sides of the fabric; however, the purl side is most common. A small-scale pattern will produce a honeycomb effect and a larger-scale pattern will produce wider, raised pattern areas.

The stitch is held in the hook of the needle until it is knitted in. The tuck loops distort the knit by pushing the stitches out of line, creating interesting patterned textures. A bumpy texture can be made by collecting loops in the needle head through tucking several rows at a time, on the same needles, before knitting in. Bear in mind that there is a limit to the number of rows that can be held on any one stitch. This depends on the tension and the type of yarn you are using. Most domestic machines are capable of holding 6–8 loops of yarn. Using extra weight and a tighter tension may help.

Selecting needles manually allows you to override the carriage and the information on the punch card or Mylar sheet, enabling you to experiment with more patterns. Tucks can also be created manually, without the use of punch cards and Mylar sheets, by taking the selected needles out of action, and setting the holding cam levers in action on the carriage. After several rows of tucking, the holding cam levers are then taken out of action and a row of plain knit is knitted. You can vary the amount of rows in hold or knit position.

Manual tuck stitch

1   Bring every third needle out into holding position. Put the holding cam levers into action on the carriage.
2   Knit three rows. Take the holding cam levers out of action. Knit one plain row.
3   Repeat the procedure. This gives you the freedom to experiment with a variety of tuck patterns.

The carriage can also be set to knit two colours at once. You can create coloured patterns by combining tuck with stripes.

1   Knit two rows in one colour, after selecting odd needles to tuck and even needles to knit.
2   Knit two rows in the second colour, tucking on odd needles and knitting on even needles.
3   Repeat the process to create a spotted pattern.

There are many variations to the basic stitch. Some interesting techniques to explore: set a punch card pattern on hold and return to plain knit every third or fourth row; this works well with vertical patterns. For a lace effect, try tucking on spaced-out needles over several rows with a tight tension and knitting plain rows in a contrasting, loose tension.

1

2

Note
On a punch card the blank spaces tuck and the punched holes knit. If you are using an electronic machine, you can mark the tuck stitches on the Mylar sheet. The result will be reversed on the machine if you select the negative option button.

1   Tuck stitch formation.
2   Shaped swatch by Zuzanna Vostiarova, showing a tuck stitch that has been worked into with hand-manipulated tucks and ripples, and holes created with partial knitting.

Lace > **Surface texture** > **Patterned knits**

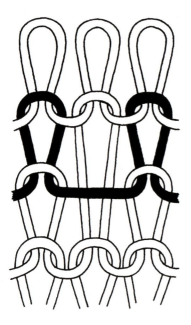
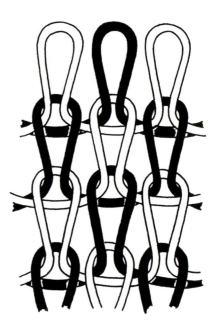

1

2

Slip stitch

Slip stitch misses the non-selected needles, allowing the yarn to lie in front of them and form 'floats'. The purl side of the work shows the texture of the pattern, with all the floats. The strands of yarns lying over the knit tend to be quite compressed, narrowing the width of the fabric and allowing very little stretch. On punch card machines, the punched holes knit and the blank spaces slip. On electronic machines, you can mark the slip stitches on the Mylar sheet and the result will be reversed if you select the negative option button.

Slip stitch is also the basis of a two-colour or Fair Isle patterning. The pattern can be knitted in two rows of each colour. If you use slip stitch in conjunction with striping, you can achieve intricate, mosaic-like patterns on the technical side of the fabric.

1–2   Slip stitch produces floats on the purl side (1) and can be used to make two-colour patterning on the reverse, technical side (2).

3   Swatch by Ruth Carpenter, which uses plating technique. Drawing inspiration from slip stitch, fabrics such as this can be created on industrial double bed machines.

Slip stitch

1   Select odd needles to knit and even needles to slip. Knit two rows of slip stitch in one colour. Note: always select the first needle in the row to knit to ensure that the floats on the purl side of the fabric are caught in to the edge of the knit.

2   Reverse the needles selected for knitting and slipping. Knit two rows of slip stitch in the second colour. The slipped stitch will rise up, elongating through the row above, forming a pattern on the technical face-side of the fabric.

3   A ripple effect can be created when the same needles are selected to slip over several rows (with a punch card set on hold), followed by a row of plain knit and then repeated.

Lace > **Surface texture** > Patterned knits

Lifting stitches

Stitches can be lifted from previously knitted rows and hung again on the needles; then, when the carriage is taken across the bed, the lifted stitches will be knitted in to the fabric, resulting in a gathered effect. This technique can be used to lift single or multiple stitches as well as floats and ladders.

To lift stitches, a transfer tool is inserted into the stitch. The tool is lifted upwards and the stitch is deposited on to a needle. This will cause the technical face-side of the fabric to pucker.

Tip
When you are starting out, wool is the easiest yarn to work with, because it has more stretch than cotton, linen or silk.

1

2

1–4   Bag designs by Justin Smith. A lifting stitch technique has been used to create different textural effects.

3

4

Random hooking up

1   Cast on as usual and knit 10 rows in the first colour.
2   Change the colour and knit 10 rows.
3   Hook up the stitches from row 10 (row 1 of the different colour) and place on the needles at random.
4   Change the colour and knit 10 rows. Repeat in different colours, hooking up where required.

Variations can include: single colour hooking up, hooking up at regular intervals to form patterns, and hooking up all the needles in a row to create horizontal ripples. Experiment with the following techniques:

1   Knit between the lifted stitches and the needles on which they are placed for a more exaggerated textural effect.
2   Create a draped effect by lifting fewer stitches and spacing them out.
3   Many more interesting textures can be made by repeating lifted stitch patterns, from carefully balanced groups of lifted stitches to irregular, distorted tucks.
4   Create a honeycomb design by alternating groups of lifted stitches with non-lifted stitches throughout the knit.
5   Lift groups of stitches to the right for a few repeats, then lift the same groups of stitches to the left for a few repeats; the result is an interesting, ruched zigzag effect.

Cables

Cables are created by crossing two groups of stitches between knitting rows. Two transfer tools are used to remove the two groups of stitches from their needles; the stitches are crossed as they are returned and then knitted as normal. Try experimenting with the number of stitches crossed and the amount of rows knitted in between.

1   Large-scale cable with foil print embellishment by Pamela Leung.

2   'Emotional Sculpture' collection by Johan Ku, made in raw wool using fingers and giant needles.

1

Lace > **Surface texture** > Patterned knits

Patterned knits

1 Fair Isle design by Alexander
   McQueen, forming part of his A/W05
   collection, entitled 'The Man Who
   Knew Too Much'.

Learning how to create patterns for knit will open up a whole range of new possibilities. Patterns such as Fair Isle and jacquard can be designed and made with a pattern card, such as a punch card or a Mylar sheet, or by using CAD. Intarsia patterns are slightly different – they can be knitted without a pattern card; they are used to create large shapes, with many colours in one row. All pattern designs are usually drawn out on graph paper first and new colour combinations worked out through trial and error on the machine.

Being able to make your own pattern cards means that you are not restricted to existing designs; it will also enable you to alter existing patterns with an experimental approach. Try exploring colours alongside different stitch designs such as tuck, slip and lace. Create elongated patterns by knitting each row twice, or by knitting a number of rows with the card locked (on hold). Alter a design by taping over selected holes, or combine sections from different cards by cutting and clipping them together. Pattern needles can be manually selected by bringing them forward before knitting each row (needle pushers are useful to push needles forward in sequence, such as 1x1 for an every-other-needle stitch pattern).

Fair Isle and jacquard

Fair Isle knitting is known for its traditional, two-colour patterns. The 'face side' has a patterned surface; the reverse side has floats of yarn, each colour passing over the other when not being knitted into the pattern. The two yarns are knitted simultaneously to produce the design on the pattern card. The reverse side of the card becomes the face side of the knit. The blank areas of the card knit the main colour; the punched areas of the card knit the contrast colour.

Traditional Fair Isles are separated by narrow borders and feature a frequent change of colour. An all-over Fair Isle design is a continual repeating pattern, with no obvious start or end; these work well with many colour combinations. Fair Isle motifs are simple designs with clean outlines and bold colours; patterns consist of lots of enclosed shapes of colour and small floats. These designs are suited to textures and tones of the same colour.

Jacquard is a double jersey knit made using a punch card or electronic machine to create a pattern. Up to four colours in a row may be used. This technique allows the floats to be knitted in at the back, creating a reversible fabric.

2

Punch cards

Punch cards provide a fast method of selecting needles, but patterns with repeats need to be worked out on paper before knitting. This is done by sketching out a rough drawing first, and then putting a stitch plan on to squared paper.

Decide on the stitch repeat size for the design; this is limited by the size of the punch card. A width of 24 needles is usual for a standard gauge machine and 30 needles for a fine gauge machine. If using a chunky gauge machine, a width of 12 needles is usual.

A design can be repeated in a number of ways to form an overall pattern, such as a drop repeat,

half-drop or step repeat. The pattern being repeated should be the correct number of stitches wide; so for example, if you are using a standard gauge machine, the width of the motif should be a number of stitches that will divide into 24 exactly – the patterns can be 2, 3, 4, 6, 8 or 12 stitches wide.

The length of the repeat can be the number of rows you choose for the design; this can be as long as the punch card will allow, or longer, if the punch cards are joined together. Work out the repeat pattern first, before filling in the whole design. Draw the design in the middle of the graph paper using the required number of needles for a repeat

pattern, then fill in the surrounding area, making sure that the repeats match up as they should. This will give you a good idea of how the overall pattern will look. Curved lines will need to be drawn as steps on the graph paper, which may alter the design slightly but alterations can be made after the sample has been knitted.

Once you have drawn the design, the graph paper template may be transferred to a punch card or a Mylar sheet. Electronic machines that use Mylar sheets are more flexible than the standard punch card machines; they are capable of producing much larger motifs and pattern repeats.

1

2

1 Patterned knit design by Cathrin Evans. The punch card clearly illustrates the pattern of the knit.

2 A series of punch cards with pattern designs.

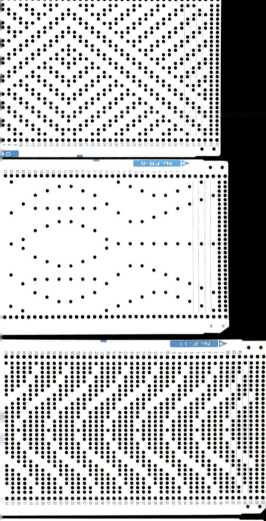

Pattern grids

For a square of knitting there are always more rows than stitches, which can make the pattern on the card seem elongated. There is special graph paper available for knitters, which consists of shorter squares to enable you to see what the finished design will look like.

Using a punch card

The position of the punch card on the needle bed is important. This is predetermined by the type and gauge of machine (standard, fine or chunky). When the card is in the machine it will automatically move one row at a time. Cards can be joined together at top and bottom with plastic clips in order to make one continuous pattern.

1. On a standard gauge Brother machine, start the pattern seven rows down. On a standard gauge Knitmaster machine, start the pattern one row down.
2. Start with the carriage to the left. Insert the card and lock it. On the carriage, change the knob to KC (knit card).
3. Thread up the main colour yarn in feeder A on a Brother machine, or feeder 1 on a Knitmaster machine.
4. Knit to the right. Release the card from being locked.
5. Select cam button(s): tuck buttons for tuck stitch; part/slip buttons for slipstitch; multicoloured /MC buttons for Fair Isle (T, S and F on a Knitmaster). Thread up with second colour in feeder B on a Brother machine, or feeder 2 on a Knitmaster. For weaving, select plain or no buttons pressed, and put weaving brushes to WT.
6. Set the row counter to 000. Carry on knitting.

Surface texture > Patterned knits

Electronic machine patterning

Domestic punch card machines have evolved from the earlier 'push button patterning' machines. Today's computerised machines have a built-in programming capacity and offer huge flexibility in patterns. Mylar sheets can be used to make patterns with larger repeats than can be achieved with the punch card method; these patterns can be repeated, reversed, turned upside down, mirror imaged, elongated in length or doubled in width.

Newer models of electronic machines, from the Brother 950i and 965i onwards, are compatible with DesignaKnit for Windows, a CAD/CAM program for knitwear design. The program covers garment pattern drafting and stitch transfer designs and it includes a graphics studio for interactive knitting and for manipulating graphics files, photographs and scanned images. The program can also be used to produce templates for punch cards and Mylar sheets, as well as charts for manual machines and hand knitters. Designers can draw stitch patterns in colour, symbols or both, and there is a range of textured stitch types to give a more realistic impression of the finished piece.

1

Industrial machine patterning

Hand-operated industrial machines are incredibly versatile, offering great possibilities for structure and pattern. They feature a patterning system that uses a high- and low-butt needle selection in combination with tuck and slip cam levers. Depending on the position of the levers, all needles might knit as normal; or low-butt needles will tuck while high-butt needles knit as normal. A similar procedure is applied to the slip technique. Patterns can be changed with each row, although the butts are not interchangeable mid-knitting; colours can be changed halfway through a row. High- and low-butt needles can be placed on the front bed only, leaving one side of the

fabric plain whilst creating ripples and stripes on the other. These machines also have a 'plating' facility, which allows a yarn to be invisible on the exterior of rib fabrics; they can be used to create fancy effects when needles are out of action or in stitch.

Today in industry modern machines, such as Shima Seiki and Stoll, do everything automatically. Individual needle selection is electronically controlled to knit coloured and textural patterns and to shape knitwear. The Shima Seiki SDS-One design system is a Windows-based system that uses three programs for knitting: one is for pattern drafting; plotting specific measurements

from the paper pattern to form the silhouette of the garment (pgm). Another is for drawing or scanning the design for the fabric surface pattern, such as jacquard (paint). The third is for creating the knit pattern; the instructions to make the structure, such as tuck, and the garment shaping information (knit paint). This package offers a visualisation of the fabric on the body; it can also illustrate the various colourways and be used to create yarn designs.

1–3 Series of designs by Amy Dyer, using the Shima Seiki design system. Illustration 3 shows from left to right: a spec drawing; a knit paint image; and a pgm image.

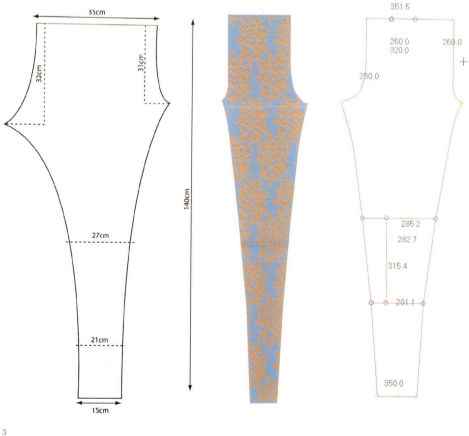

1

1–3   Intarsia designs by Hannah Taylor.
        Photography by Jojo Ma.

2

3

Intarsia

Intarsia is a technique used for colour patterning in which there are no floats, as each colour is separately knitted in to its own shape. Many colours can be knitted into one row and because there are no floats, large, bold pattern shapes can be made. Special intarsia carriages are available for the more sophisticated machines. Always start with needles at intarsia position: latches open and needles forward about 1cm (2/5in). This is usually achieved by a pass of the empty intarsia carriage.

Intarsia technique

1   A ball of yarn is required for each pattern shape; place them on the floor in front of the machine.
2   Place the end of each coloured yarn across the open latches of the groups of needles in the pattern order for the row, with the short end nearest to the carriage and yarns crossing under needles.
3   Take the intarsia carriage across the needles to knit the row; each separate colour will knit with its own needles.
4   Repeat the procedure, manually placing the yarns back across the needles in the order required for each row, crossing under needles as before.
5   Knit one row and continue.

Surface texture > Patterned knits

'Fashion is a lot closer to the body, not just the form, but also the movement.'

Hussein Chalayan

1   'Elizabeth' dress by Jemma Sykes
     for ethical label Butcher Couture,
     hand-knitted in organic wool.

In Chapter 4 the knitted swatch is transformed into a three-dimensional piece. There are a number of different shaping methods, such as draping and shaping on a mannequin to create silhouettes. There are exercises to show you how to plan shapes on paper (pattern cutting) and how to transfer these outlines into knit patterns. You will be guided through the shaping of a basic bodice and sleeve pattern, with detailed instructions for stitches and rows. Finally, there is a detailed section that explains how to create three-dimensional effects, such as frills and flared pieces, straight from the machine.

Partial knitting: three-dimensional effects

1   Partial knitting / holding technique
    was used in these swatches by
    Natalie Osborne.
2   Chart showing knitting a diagonal
    join between two colours using
    holding technique.
3   Holding technique used in
    combination with different weights
    of yarn. Design by Juliana Sissons.

Partial knitting can be used to create a variety of three-dimensional effects: fabric texture, sculptural surfaces and unusual silhouettes; diagonal blocks of colour, flared skirt panels and even slanting shoulder shapes; as well as interesting edges, such as looped or scalloped effects.

The holding cam controls are set on hold. Needles on the opposite side of the bed from the carriage are manually put into holding position. Groups of needles can be put in to holding position all at once, or needles can be held one at a time. This technique allows the carriage to pass over these needles without knitting the stitches in; however, when these needles are put back into working position the stitches will resume knitting as normal. Other needles that are not in holding position will continue to knit rows, accumulating length. It is important to keep your weights under the working needles and move them up the fabric as it grows.

1

Short row patterning

Designs based on diagonal and horizontal lines can enable a change of stitch size or colour within a single row. You can create a slanting edge by putting needles on hold, gradually. A line of small lace holes will appear between the two sections, which can enhance the look of the design. However, this can be avoided by wrapping the free yarn under the first held needle each time the carriage arrives at the point where the working needles meet the holding needles and before knitting the next row.

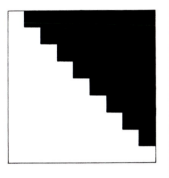

2

Knitting a diagonal join

1 Always start with the carriage at the opposite end of the needles that are going to be brought into hold. Thread up the first colour and cast on approximately 60 stitches.
2 Knit several rows in plain knitting, finishing with the carriage on the left.
3 Set the holding cam levers on hold. Bring the first needle on the right-hand side to holding position and knit one row. Take the free yarn under the held needle and knit the next row. Bring the second needle on the right to holding position and knit a row. Take the free yarn under the second held needle and over the first. Knit the next row. Repeat the process until there is only one needle still knitting. Bring this needle to holding position.
4 Unthread the yarn from the feeder and take the empty carriage across to the other side (the carriage has to be moved to the side of the bed on which the first needle was brought out of hold).
5 Thread up the second colour. The next section is knitted by pushing the needles back into working position. Using a transfer tool, return the first needle on the right-hand side to working position and knit two rows. Bring the second needle on the right to working position and knit two rows. Repeat the process until there is only one needle still in holding position. Bring this needle to working position.

Note: when bringing needles into holding position, lace holes will form along the diagonal line if you do not take the free yarn under the held needle each time.

To achieve variation in the depth of angle, experiment by bringing two or more needles out at a time or by knitting more rows between these held needles. Also try striping with different coloured yarns to clearly show the short-row patterning.

3

Three-dimensional effects

You can knit separate sections of fabric by putting groups of needles into holding position at various times, which allows you to change the colour, stitch size and so on.

1 This chart illustrates knitting a raised pattern within the fabric, using groups of needles in holding position. The knitted sections are worked individually, with all other needles on hold. The held needles change as each separate section is knitted.

2–5 Swatches of three-dimensional knit by Victoria Hill.

Knitting a raised pattern

1 Hold the groups of needles and then put them back into working position, either all at once or gradually, one at a time. Repeat the pattern to create three-dimensional, sculptured surfaces.

2 Two halves of a knitted piece can be worked separately, resulting in a vertical slit between the two, which can either be sewn together later or left open for design purposes (such as for buttonholes).

3 Try holding all needles on the left whilst knitting 30 rows on the right; then hold all needles on the right whilst knitting 30 rows on the left. Both sets of needles will have knitted 30 rows and knitting can resume as normal with all needles in working position. If one group of needles is held longer than the other group, allowing more rows to occur on one side, you will create an interesting loop of knitting. Try knitting and holding alternate blocks of needles to form an overall looped fabric, which will provide exciting new starting points for design developments. The longer the needles are held, the bigger the raised sections tend to be.

1

2

3

4

5

Creating flared shapes

Fullness in shaped garments, such as those with frills or flare, is often achieved by inserting triangular godets. These godets can be knitted horizontally at any length or width required. Tiny ruffles can be achieved just as easily as a full-length flare. These can be knitted in continuously with the use of the partial knitting technique.

1

Making a frilled edge

1. Start with the carriage on the right-hand side. The frill will be made on the left-hand edge. Thread up the yarn and cast on the required amount of stitches. Knit 21 rows of plain knitting, finishing with the carriage on the left.
2. Set the holding cam levers to hold. Bring all needles on the right-hand side to hold, apart from 20 needles on the left (this will form the length of frill).
3. Knit two rows. Bring the first needle on the right-hand side to holding position and knit two rows. Bring the second needle on the right-hand side to holding position and knit two rows.
   Repeat the process until there is only one needle still knitting. Bring this needle to hold position.
4. Take the holding cam levers off hold to resume normal knitting. Knit two rows, ending with carriage on the left-hand side.
5. Repeat steps 3 and 4 to produce a triangular godet, which will have lace holes outlining the edges.
6. Take the holding cam levers off hold to resume normal knitting. Knit 20 rows of plain knitting, finishing with the carriage on the left.
7. Repeat the entire process from the beginning until you have created enough godets to result in a frilly edge along the left-hand side of the knit.

Experiment with the length and width of the godets by changing the number of stitches and rows.

A singular spiral frill can be made in the same way. Knit only the length of the godet and repeat the process to create a circular shape; if you continue further, a spiral frill will be made.

2

3

4

5

Partial knitting: three-dimensional effects > **Creating flared shapes** > Increasing and decreasing

Flared skirts

1 Illustration showing panel of skirt with two inserted godets.

2 Flared cape by Dulcie Wanless. This is a good example of the use of godets for adding flare and shape.

Flared skirts can be knitted sideways using the frilled edge technique (on the previous page). It can be knitted in one continuous piece; for example, to make a skirt to fit a 66cm waist, you would need to divide this measurement into the number of panels required. If six panels are required (66cm divided by 6 = 11cm), each panel will need to measure 11cm at the waist edge. To convert to imperial, 1cm = 2/5in.

1 Knit a tension swatch to calculate the number of rows in an 11cm length.

2 Cast on the number of stitches for the required length of skirt (this can be calculated from the tension swatch). The length of the skirt will be restricted by the length of the machine bed; remember that you are knitting sideways. Knit enough rows to measure 5.5cm (half a panel).

3 Set the holding cam levers to hold. Add a godet the full length of the skirt. The width of the godet will depend on how many needles you put on holding position each time and how many rows you knit in between. For example, holding one needle every two rows will give you a fuller godet than holding five needles every two rows; knitting five rows between each hold will give you a fuller godet than knitting two rows between each hold.

4 Take the holding cam levers off hold to resume normal knitting. Knit the other half of the panel, enough rows to measure 5.5cm. This completes one panel.

5 Repeat the process another five times. The waist edge will end up measuring 66cm and the hem edge will have flare.

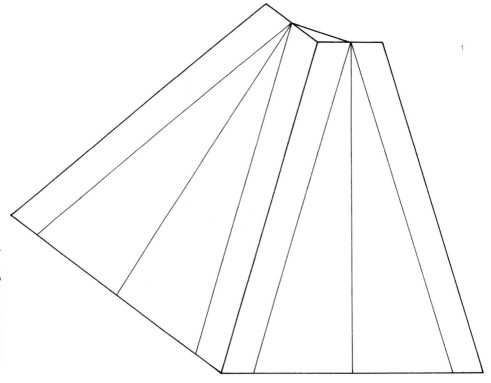

1

2

Increasing and decreasing

A single stitch or many stitches can be transferred in one move by using a transfer tool. This movement increases or decreases the total number of stitches being knitted. Shaping can be used on an outside edge or to form darts within the body of the knit.

Shaping by 'fully fashioning' involves transferring groups of stitches at the edge of the fabric. When decreasing or narrowing the shape, a group of stitches is moved in one go; the inner-most stitch of the group is placed on top of the stitch adjacent to it, thus losing one needle at the edge. You must remember to push this edge needle into non-working position to avoid it knitting back in with the next row. It is also possible to move the stitches two or three needle spaces across, losing two or three needles at the edge. Repeating this action along the outer edge of a knit creates a wale line, a neat characteristic of fully fashioning.

When increasing stitches outwards (making the knitted piece wider), a space is created adjacent to the inner-most needle of the group being moved, which leaves an eyelet hole in the knit. Knitting in this way will form a line of eyelets on the edge; these can form a decorative trim as part of the design or they can be filled in by moving a stitch up on to the empty needle from the previous row. To increase by more than one stitch at a time, put the required number of needles into working position and cast on using the e-wrap method in the normal way.

These transfers are also used to create eyelet designs for decorative trims. When a single-stitch transfer is used, the stitch can be placed on top of the stitch of its adjacent needle, to be knitted together in the next row; or it can be placed on to the empty needle on the outside of the knit, forming an eyelet when the next two rows are knitted. Note: if the empty needle is put into non-working position, a ladder will form.

On a double bed machine it is possible to transfer stitches from one bed to the other using a bodkin, which has an eyelet at each end, making it easier to transfer a stitch from one bed to the other.

1

2

Decreasing by holding stitches

Shoulders and other shallow angles can be shaped by using the holding technique (partial knitting). The holding cam levers are set on hold and each shoulder is shaped in turn. The carriage should be on the opposite side to the shoulder being shaped. The needles are brought into holding position gradually, working in from the outside edge (for example, two needles every second row) until the shaping is finished. Each shoulder can then be cast off separately in the normal way.

1   Knitwear design by Juliana Sissons. The shaped bodice panels have been darted and fully fashioned. A holding technique has been used to create different length slashes and circular hip panels.

Shaping a vertical dart

Vertical darts can be found within the body of a garment, such as on a shaped neckline or skirt.

1   Thread up the machine and cast on the desired amount of stitches. Knit several rows.
2   Transfer the centre stitch on to its adjacent left needle, leaving an empty needle in the middle.
3   Use a transfer tool to move the next three stitches on the right by one space to the left. Repeat this action until all the stitches on the right are transferred to the left. This will leave an empty needle on the far right. Put the needle into non-working position.
4   Repeat the process every four or five rows, until you have completed the required amount of shaping. More than one dart can be manoeuvred at the same time, within the body of knit. An adjustable multi-head transfer tool is useful for this or a garter bar can be used.

Shaping a horizontal dart

1   Thread up the machine and cast on the desired amount of stitches. Knit several rows, finishing with the carriage on the right.
2   Set the holding cam levers on to hold. Bring the first two needles on the left to holding position and knit two rows. Bring the next two needles on the left to holding position and knit two rows. Continue until 20 needles are held and the carriage is on the right-hand side.
3   Take the holding cam levers off hold and resume normal knitting. The width and length of the resulting dart is dependent on the number of needles put on hold and the number of rows knitted.

1

Draping and shaping

1   Flat pattern cutting on dot
    and cross paper.
2   Basic bodice blocks in card.

The mannequin plays an important role in the shape-making process. Blocks, patterns and knitted pieces can all be checked and fitted on the form. Blocks can also be moulded straight on to the mannequin, without the use of paper drafts, for quicker visual results; this is often a preferred method of pattern cutting for the beginner. However, the best results are gained through a combination of flat pattern cutting and modelling on the stand, and it is important to have a knowledge and understanding of both.

1

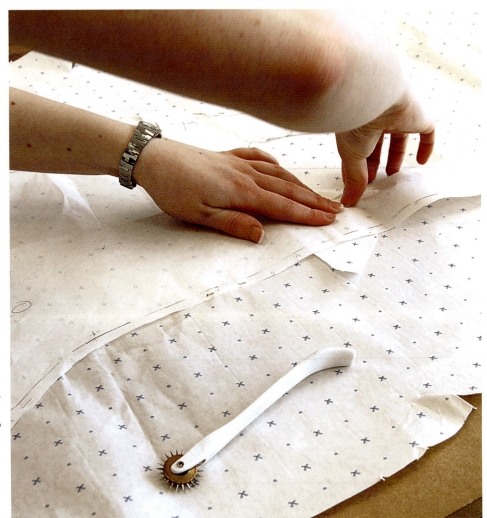

Block patterns

In flat pattern cutting a basic block pattern is first drafted to fit a standard-size figure. The block is used by designers as a foundation for new styles, pleats, tucks, godets and gathers; it can be adapted into many design variations whilst still retaining the original size and fit.

Different types of garments require specific basic blocks, so for example, the dartless bodice block and the over-garment block, both of which have more ease than a basic fitted bodice block, are more suitable for jacket or coat designs and can be adapted to have an even easier fit. Dress blocks can have the ease reduced to make them suitable for lingerie styles. Stretch blocks have a tighter fit and can be a good starting point for certain knitwear designs. See how to make a block pattern on page 122.

Patterns for knit

Bodice blocks used for knit fabrics are different to those used for woven materials. They have no darts, are slightly tighter and, due to the nature of the stretch fabric, they have no seam allowances added. Each designer or company will use blocks that they have personally adapted to suit their particular style of knitwear.

After the block has been developed into a designed pattern the knitting pattern can be calculated. The pattern contains the number of stitches and rows in each section, calculated by taking all the horizontal and vertical measurements in the pattern, as well as using the knitted tension swatch.

Knitted samples and part-garment trials can be made to test the stretch of the knit against the stretch of the toile. The knitted pieces are likely to vary from the toile pieces and will need to be adjusted, usually through trial and error, until a perfect fit is achieved. See how to make a knitting pattern on page 123.

Knitted samples

Finished patterns are made up as jersey toiles for knitted fabric designs. The toile is used to check the design lines, proportion and fit before the design is made up into the final fabric or developed into a pattern for knit. After the first sample garment is complete, the design is ready to show to buyers and, if orders are received, the pattern is graded up into the sizes required. The British Standards Institution publishes tables of sizes, which are used by manufacturers as a guide when grading up or down from their standard size.

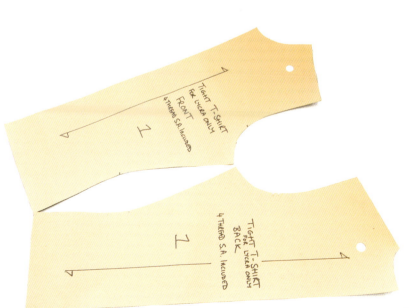

Increasing and decreasing > Draping and shaping > Creating a knitting pattern

Using a mannequin

Modelling on the stand opens up a certain freedom and spontaneity with three-dimensional design. Fluid jerseys can be pinned at strategic points to produce fullness in the form of cowls and drapes. Large knitted shapes can be wrapped around the mannequin to create interesting grain and seam lines and jersey toile fabrics then moulded into the negative spaces, in order to create pattern shapes for the missing parts.

It is important to be able to make your design readable so that it can be transferred to a pattern. All the vertical and horizontal markings from the mannequin should be drawn on to the toile fabric, such as centre front, centre back and side seams, as well as the chest, bust, armhole, waist- and hip-lines. All darts, tucks, pleats and fold lines should also be carefully marked, along with balance points; matching instruction notes, such as 'point A to A' and 'B to B', are particularly useful when working on complicated draped designs.

After the design has been completed on the stand, measurements have to be checked and made accurate. All side seams and joining style lines, whether they are straight or curved, need to match in length. This is difficult to achieve by pinning to the stand alone.

Note: only drape with a toile fabric that has a similar weight and thickness as the fabric in which the final design will be made.

Padding the stand

Stands can be padded to obtain different measurements; this is useful when making for individual clients, especially if figures are uneven in any way. A small deficiency is made up with wadding and held in place with strips of calico. For a larger alteration a calico bodice block is made from a drafted pattern to the required size. The stand is padded with small layers of wadding and built up gradually to fit the toile. The thickness is graded around the bust, calico strips are used to keep the wadding in place, and then the toile is fitted over the top.

Draped necklines

Draped necklines are created by inserting a triangle shape, similar to a godet. A v-shaped neckline can be drafted on the basic bodice block pattern, about 1–3cm away from the neck edge. The triangular shape is drafted on paper separately; its outside edges should be the same length as the neckline edge. The centre line of the triangle is slashed down to the point and pivoted open. The pattern is then redrawn along the top edge to include the fuller shape; this top edge width will give you the depth of the front drape on the neckline. Experiment with this basic technique to achieve different lengths and fullness of drape. You can also drape jersey toile fabric directly on the stand for a quicker visual result.

Another way to achieve a draped neckline effect is to knit the body vertically, using partial knitting (see page 102). Decide on the depth and width of the top of the triangle first (to achieve the shape and size of the drape) and then calculate the pattern by holding the required number of needles over the required number of rows.

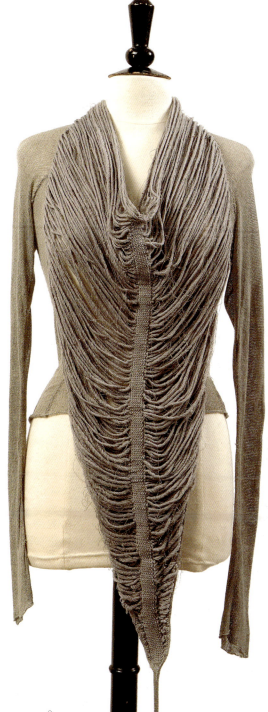

1   Jersey toiles can be pinned at points on the stand to produce a draped neckline.

2   Draped design by Juliana Sissons, using ladder technique. Fine linen yarn was used in combination with soft, bouncy acrylic.

2

Increasing and decreasing > **Draping and shaping** > Creating a knitting pattern

Basic bodice form

Only one side of the stand is used, unless developing asymmetrical designs, in which case both sides of the mannequin are used.

1   Prepare a piece of toile fabric 10cm longer than the back length (nape-to-waist measurement) and wide enough to cover half of the back.
2   Pin the straight grain down the centre back, with about 5cm above the neckline and 5cm below the waistline.
3   Hold the fabric straight across the width of the back to the armhole and pin in place at the underarm (make sure the grain of the fabric is straight).
4   Work from the centre back neck, a little at a time, cutting and marking the fitting lines of the neck, shoulder and armhole.
5   If using a stretch toile fabric, work outwards from the centre back to smooth the fullness in the back waist. Mark in the side lines and waistline. Pin to stand and cut off surplus fabric, leaving about 2cm for turning. If using calico toile fabric, keep the grain straight, mark in the side lines and pin to stand. Pin and mark the dart from the waistline where the fold of fabric appears. Pin and mark waistline and cut off surplus fabric, leaving about 2cm for turning.
6   For the front, prepare the toile fabric in the same way as for the back. Pin the straight grain down the centre front, with about 5cm above the neckline and 5cm below the waistline.
7   Hold the fabric straight across the bust line, pin to hold at the underarm point, keeping the grain of the fabric straight.
8   Working round the neck and shoulder, pin, mark and cut off excess fabric, matching to the back shoulder. If using a stretch toile fabric, work from the centre front outwards to smooth the fullness in the shoulder and armhole; mark and pin. If using calico toile fabric, keep the grain straight, mark and pin a dart in the centre of the shoulder down to the bust point. Smooth out at the armhole, mark and pin.
9   Adjust and pin under the arm to the back side seam. If using stretch toile fabric, work from the centre front to smooth out as much fullness as possible in to the side seam in order to avoid creating a waist dart; mark and pin side seam and waist line. Cut off surplus fabric, leaving about 2cm for turning. If using calico toile fabric, pin under the arm to back side seam, pin and mark dart at waistline, where the fold of fabric appears. Pin and mark waistline. Cut off surplus fabric, leaving about 2cm for turning.

Note: the measurements here are in metric. To convert to imperial, 1cm = 2/5in.

1–4   Here, jersey has been pinned to the stand through the centre-front line. It has been smoothed over the shoulder and pinned under the armhole. The neck and armhole have then been cut away to form a bodice shape.

1

2

3

4

Creating a knitting pattern

1–3   Selection of vintage knitting patterns.

There are a number of things to consider before commencing a pattern. For your first attempt, it would be best to work on a simple garment that requires little shaping. Ribbed bands, such as hems, cuffs and neck bands and so on, must be able to stretch and fit close to the body. To calculate the number of stitches needed to make the rib, calculate the width of the part of garment it is being attached to. When the rib is knitted on to this edge, it will automatically pull in the fabric to fit close to the body.

Stretch will differ in each knitted piece, depending on the yarn, tension and knitting technique used. The starting point is the tension swatch. Knit a number of tension swatches until you have achieved the desired look and feel of the fabric. A swatch should be made for each yarn and pattern technique used.

Sketch the garment to help you calculate the knitting pattern; this drawing need not to be to scale but should give all width and length measurements. Add an extra 5cm (2in) in the width to allow for ease (unless the design is close-fitting, in which case less ease is needed).

Measurements

Whenever possible, take the actual body measurements of the person you are knitting for, unless you are making garments to a standard size. The following measurements are required for a basic bodice block.

- Bust: measure around the fullest part of the bust (standard size 88cm)
- Nape to waist: measure from the bone at the back of the neck to the natural waistline. Extra length can be added as desired (standard size 40cm)
- Armhole depth: measure from the shoulder point to the underarm point at the side seam. This measurement can vary depending on the desired length (standard size 21cm)
- Neck size: measure around the base of the neck (standard size 37cm)
- Shoulder: measure from the base of neck to the shoulder point (standard size 12.5cm)
- Back width: measure across the back from the point of underarm to underarm (standard size 34.5cm)
- Arm length: measure from the shoulder point to the wrist, over a slightly bent arm (standard size 58.5cm)
- Top arm: measure around the fullest part of the upper arm. This measurement can vary depending on desired effect (standard size 28.5cm)
- Wrist: standard size 18cm (make sure the wrist measurement allows for stretch over a clenched fist)

Note: the measurements here are in metric. To convert to imperial, 1cm = 2/5in.

2

3

Draping and shaping > Creating a knitting pattern

Basic block with classic set-in sleeve

Draft a standard stretch block from the measurements on page 121. You can add more ease in the bust and armhole depth as required and 5cm or more to the top arm measurement. To create a closer fitting, higher armhole, reduce the armhole depth by around 2–3cm. The length of the bodice and sleeve can also be varied.

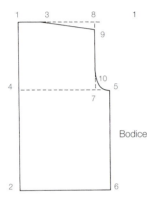

Bodice

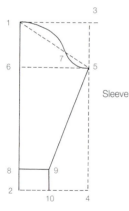

Sleeve

1   Simple pattern guide for basic block with classic set-in sleeve.

2–3   A simple, basic bodice knit block and sleeve, which have allowances for ease. Both include measurements as well as the calculated stitches and rows.

4   This illustration of the front neckline shows stitches and rows using a tension sample of 3 stitches and 4 rows to 1cm.

Front and back bodice

1   1–2 Nape to waist. Square across from 1 and 2.
2   1–3 One fifth of neck measurement.
3   1–4 Armhole depth plus depth of shoulder slope (for example, 3cm).
4   4–5 Square across by quarter bust measurement.
5   5–6 Square down to 6, to meet line from 2.
6   4–7 Half of the back width measurement .
7   7–8 Square up from 7 to meet line from 1.
8   8–9 Shoulder slope depth (for example, 3cm). Join 3 to 9.
9   5–10 Draw curve touching the line from 4, for approximately 3cm. You now have half a back bodice.
10 Draw in front neckline on top of the drafted back bodice, from 3 as required (make sure that the combined front and back neck measurements are not less than half the neck size).
11 Trace off bodice with front neckline to achieve two separate pattern pieces: the half front and the half back bodice.

Set-in sleeve

1   1–2 Sleeve length. Square across from 1 and 2.
2   1–3 Half top arm measurement. Square down to meet the line from 2.
3   1–5 Draw a line from 1, which is the measurement of the armhole depth, to touch the line from 3 to 4.
4   5–6 Square across from 5 to 6 on the line from 1 to 2.
5   5–7 One third of length of 5 to 1; use this point to direct sleeve head curve.
6   5–1 Draw in curve touching the line from 6 for approximately 3cm, through point 7 to finish at 1. Make sure that the length of the sleeve head is the same measurement as the armhole on the bodice (you may need to adjust the curve in order to get the correct measurement).
7   2–8 Cuff depth. This can be any measurement you choose, depending on the design. Square across (from 8–9) by half the cuff width, bearing in mind the wrist measurement.
8   9–10 Square down to the line from 2 to 4. Join 9 to 5.
9   This gives you half the sleeve. The other half is mirrored from the centre sleeve length line.
10 Once the bodice and sleeve blocks have ben drafted, a 1cm seam allowance can be added to all outside edges. Make a stretch jersey toile to check size and proportions. At this point, the width of the waist can be narrowed and fitted along the side seams.

Knitting pattern for a basic block

This simple body pattern is intended to illustrate the general principle of calculating a knitting pattern; the shape is just a starting point and can be adapted to alter the style. Shoulders may be sloped, the sleeve head and armhole may be shaped and necklines varied.

All the width and length measurements are written on the drawing of the garment. This simple shape shows front and back body and a square sleeve. The sleeve head is double the armhole depth measurement (for example, 19 x 2 = 38cm). This example uses an estimated front neck depth of 10cm. The back neck is straight across the back.

The next stage is to work out the knitting pattern using the tension square measurements. This example uses a tension measurement of 3 stitches and 4 rows to 1cm.

Note: all the measurements here are in metric. To convert to imperial, 1cm = 2/5in.

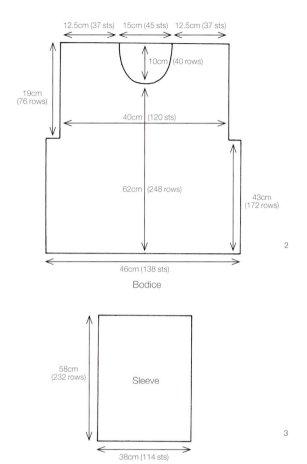

12.5cm (37 sts)   15cm (45 sts)   12.5cm (37 sts)

10cm (40 rows)

19cm (76 rows)

40cm (120 sts)

62cm (248 rows)

43cm (172 rows)

46cm (138 sts)

Bodice

2

58cm (232 rows)

Sleeve

38cm (114 sts)

3

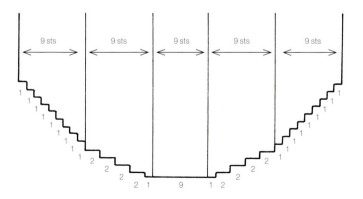

9 sts   9 sts   9 sts   9 sts   9 sts

4

Knitting the pattern

1. Cast on 138 stitches.
2. Knit 172 rows.
3. Cast off 9 stitches on each side.
4. Knit 36 rows. The front neckline will begin to be knitted from this row. If knitting the back, continue for another 40 rows and cast off.
5. Front neckline: divide the neck width (45 sts) into 5 equal parts (9 sts).
6. Put the carriage at the right-hand side (120 sts on the bed).
7. Put 61 left-hand needles on hold.
8. Hold 5 right-hand side centre needles. Knit 2 rows.
9. Hold 2 right-hand side centre needles. Knit 2 rows. Repeat 3 times.
10. Hold 1 right-hand side centre needle. Knit 2 rows. Repeat 8 times.
11. For the next 12 rows knit straight.
12. Cast off the right shoulder. The shoulder should have 37.5 stitches, but as a half stitch is not possible, the number is either rounded up to 38 stitches or down to 37 stitches per shoulder. This can be adjusted at the neck edge and, because the fabric is stretchy, one stitch will make very little difference to the fit of the neckline.
13. Put the 61 stitches on the left-hand side back into action using a transfer tool.
14. Re-thread yarn and put the carriage to the left-hand side of bed.
15. Hold 6 left-hand side centre needles. Knit 2 rows.
16. Hold 2 left-hand side centre needles. Knit 2 rows. Repeat 3 more times.
17. Hold 1 left-hand side centre needle. Knit 2 rows. Repeat 8 times.
18. Knit 12 rows straight.
19. Cast off the left shoulder.
20. Put all needles back into working position with a transfer tool and cast off remaining stitches.
21. Sleeve: cast on 114 stitches and knit 232 rows. Cast off.

1–2   Designs by Natalie Osborne, showing different neckline styles.

Calculation of stitches and rows

Calculating stitches and rows is very important for making up a garment; you will often need to shape diagonal or slanting style lines, such as for necklines, shoulders, armholes and sleeves. All shaped pieces are basically calculated in the same way: divide the number of stitches that need to be decreased by the number of rows you need to knit them in; this will give you the number of rows to be knitted between each decrease action.

Neckline shaping

Most necklines are worked in a similar way, often part-working in the middle and then knitting both sides separately according to shape; whilst working on one side, the other side is put on hold. Alternatively, waste yarn can be knitted on to the side that is not being shaped first: this takes the knitting off the machine for a while and can be useful when working in particularly fine yarns, as it avoids the carriage having to go many times over the held needles. One of the simplest styles is the square neckline, where the centre stitches are simply cast off, then each side is separately knitted straight up.

For a round neckline, you will need to check that the overall measurement is correct; if not, the shape will need to be adjusted to fit. The back neck can often be knitted straight but for finer knitting it is better to have a slight curve. The round neck can be easily converted to a V-neck by drawing in the style line down from the neck point to the centre-front line. Both of these neckline styles are suitable for a variety of collar designs to be attached (see collars and neckbands on page 132).

Abbreviation
Stitch(es) = st(s)

1

When knitting a V-neck, you will need to bring out half of the needles on the opposite side to the carriage into holding position, so they do not knit. Shape the 'V' by bringing the required number of needles into hold every alternate row (or according to the pattern calculations). Continue in this way until only the required number of stitches for the shoulder is left in working position. After completing one side and casting off the shoulder, the other side can be worked.

2

Shoulder shaping

A set-in sleeve must have a sloping shoulder line. Shoulders are shaped by putting needles into holding position on alternate rows, from the armhole edge on the opposite side to the carriage.

To calculate the shoulder slant, draw a horizontal line on the paper pattern, from the outside, lower shoulder point, inwards towards the neck; then a vertical line up from here to touch the neck edge. The vertical line will give you the measurement for the height of the slant and the number of rows that need to be knitted. The horizontal line will give you the length of the shoulder and the number of stitches that need to be put on hold. Divide the number of rows into the number of stitches to calculate the number of needles to be held on alternate rows. When the shaping is complete, the holding needles are put back into working position with a transfer tool. One row can be knitted before casting off (if the seam is to be grafted later, you will need to knit off with waste yarn).

A straight or dropped shoulder requires no shaping. Often the neck and shoulder lines are knitted all in one with the back. If a slash neckline is required, the front neckline can also be knitted in one with the shoulder line.

Armhole shaping

To knit an armhole, you will need to calculate how many stitches are to be decreased and how many rows it will take to decrease this number of stitches.

To decrease inwards 5cm over a height of 8cm, first refer to your tension swatch. This example is 3.7 rows and 3.3 stitches in a 1cm square:

8cm x 3.7 = 29.6
(approximately 30 rows)

5cm x 3.3 = 16.5
(approximately 16 stitches)

30 divide by 16 = 1.87 (approximately 2)

16 stitches need to be decreased over 30 rows. Therefore, one stitch can be decreased/fully fashioned inwards every 2 rows for 30 rows, before continuing to knit straight.

Remember to shape both sides at the same time in order to achieve symmetrical shaping but also remember that knitting is extensible, so rounding the calculations up or down makes it easier for you without altering the desired shape.

For a rounder armhole shape, try casting off a number of stitches at the start of the shaping. You will need to alternate the start of shaping from one armhole to the other as the carriage must begin on the same side as the armhole being decreased. So, the right-hand side armhole will be started on one row of knitting and the left-hand side armhole will be started on the next row of knitting.

Note: the measurements here are in metric. To convert to imperial, 1cm = 2/5in.

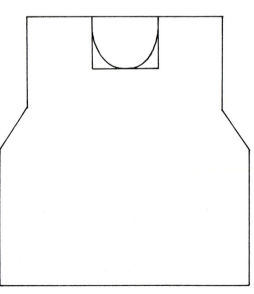

Simple armhole

1 Cast off 5 stitches at armhole side.

2 Knit 2 rows and decrease 2 stitches at armhole side.

3 Knit 2 more rows and decrease 2 stitches at armhole side.

4 Knit 2 rows and decrease 1 stitch at armhole side. Repeat 3 times.

5 Knit 6 rows and decrease 1 stitch. Repeat.

6 This gives you armhole shaping of approximately 5cm/2/5in (15 stitches and 24 rows). Knit straight to the shoulder point and cast off.

Sleeve pattern

The crown of the sleeve must correspond with the armhole shape in order to fit correctly: a square or slit-style armhole will require a rectangular shaped sleeve; a shaped armhole will require a shaped sleeve head. All sleeve patterns can be adapted to be straight, narrow or flared.

1   Sleeve pattern with example tension of 4 rows and 3 stitches per 1cm square.

2   Sleeve crown with example tension of 4 rows and 3 stitches per 1cm square.

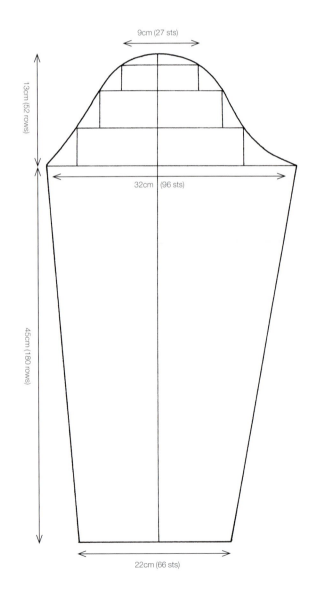

9cm (27 sts)

13cm (52 rows)

32cm (96 sts)

45cm (180 rows)

1

22cm (66 sts)

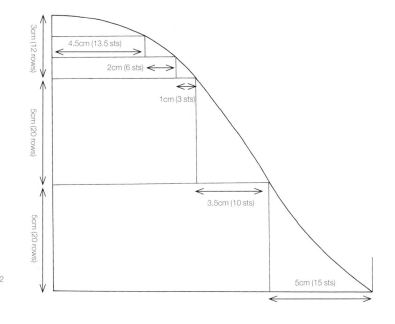

3cm (12 rows)

4.5cm (13.5 sts)

2cm (6 sts)

1cm (3 sts)

5cm (20 rows)

3.5cm (10 sts)

5cm (20 rows)

2

5cm (15 sts)

Sleeve pattern

The sample tension for this exercise is 4 rows and 3 stitches per 1cm square – refer to illustrations 1 and 2.

1 Draw a line down the centre of the sleeve pattern and mark the horizontal and vertical measurements.
2 Divide the sleeve head into sections, according to the curve of the crown – this will make shaping easier (see illustration 1).
3 Calculate the number of rows and stitches for each measurement (see illustration 2).
4 Cast on 66 stitches. Knit 180 rows, increasing 1 stitch on each side every 12 rows (calculated as follows: 30 extra stitches needed, 15 on each side; 180 divided by 15 = 12).
5 The following instructions apply to both sides of the sleeve. To begin the sleeve crown we have to decrease 15 stitches over 20 rows (20 divided by 15 = 1.3). We cannot decrease every 1.3 rows so, in this case, you could cast off 5 stitches and then decrease 1 stitch every 2 rows. Alternatively, decrease 1 stitch every row for the first 10 rows, then decrease 1 stitch every 2 rows for the final 10 rows.

6 For the next part of the sleeve crown, decrease 10 stitches over 20 rows (20 divided by 10 = 2). This allows you to simply decrease 1 stitch every 2 rows
7 The final part of the sleeve crown is divided into three 1cm sections. For section one, decrease 3 stitches over 4 rows (knit 1 row, then decrease 1 stitch every row for 3 rows).
8 For section two, decrease 6 stitches over 4 rows (you could decrease 1 stitch each row for 2 rows and then 2 stitches each row for 2 rows).
9 For section three, decrease 13 stitches over 4 rows One way of doing this is to decrease 3 stitches every row for 3 rows, then leave the final 4 stitches to be cast off. The final part of shaping can be achieved by holding needles and then casting off. If you are decreasing more than two stitches at once, you may find it easier if you cast off these stitches instead of decreasing them.

Note: the measurements here are in metric. To convert to imperial, 1cm = 2/5in.

Draping and shaping > **Creating a knitting pattern**

1   Necklace by Elinor Voytal. Elinor
        makes statement jewellery pieces
        using machine-knitted silk and
        viscose and intricate embellishment
        with metal and crystal.

'With all the stripes of pink and blue, Hold sweet thoughts
to weave in, too; Over and under, through and through,
Hold them fast and weave them true.'

L. Glaiser Foster

The finishing of a knitted piece is an important consideration
and can make or break the look of a garment. Details such
as trims, edges and fastenings should be considered at the
design stage, and not left as an afterthought.

This chapter examines collars and neckbands, hems and
edges, pockets and fastenings. It also looks at hand-finishing
techniques, such as blocking, pressing and seams. Finally, it
looks at embroidery and embellishment, with a handy section
on beading and beading stitches.

Collars and neckbands

1 Chunky rib roll collar by Julia Neill.
2 Designs by Victoria Hill, featuring ruffled neck (left) and polo neck (right).

Collars generally extend the line of the garment neck; neckbands follow the line of the neck edge. Both collars and neckbands may be knitted directly on to a garment or knitted and attached separately. Depending on the shape and style of the design, they can be knitted horizontally or vertically and can be plain knit, ribbed, lace, patterned or have a fancy style edging such as picot.

1

Neckbands

Polo necks and crew necks are common styles based on the neckband principle. A polo neck is a simple rectangle of ribbed knit, turned over at the top. In order to sit correctly, the under part (the part nearest to the neck edge) can be knitted at a slightly tighter tension than the outer part (the part folded over). Polo necks fit round the neck better if they are of rib construction; therefore the tension must be established separately from the body. The crew neck is also a ribbed piece, but this is not turned over and sits lower around the neck, as the back and front necklines have the same shape. These bands stretch to fit and are joined at one shoulder seam.

Neckbands for V-necks are sometimes shaped at the centre front so that the ends meet in the middle. Bands for square necklines are made in several pieces and joined by overlapping the ends, which is an easier method of finishing.

Ribbed neckbands and collars need to be elastic enough to go over the head but still fit correctly at the neck edge. Measure the neck edge and calculate the number of stitches required based on the

tension swatches for the garment. The neckband can be knitted with a slightly smaller stitch size for a tighter fit. If the neckline was knitted off on waste yarn, the stitches can be hooked back on to the machine in order to make the collar.

2

Collars

There are three main types of collar: flat collars, which include the Peter Pan, Eton and sailor; stand collars, such as the mandarin, polo and shirt collar; and grown-on collars (which are knitted in one with the garment) such as rever, roll and reefer styles. All these shapes can be developed into a variety of frilled collars, using a simple pattern cutting technique.

Collars may be knitted in various ways. One method is to knit the collar horizontally, in plain or patterned knit, on a single bed machine. The collar can be folded in half to make a double thickness and it can be shaped in to the fold line and back out to the neck edge, or vice-versa, depending on the style.

Another way is to knit the collar horizontally on a double bed machine and keep it as a single thickness; this method lends itself well to shaping possibilities. Either of these collar types can be knitted on to the neckline by picking up the neck edge of the garment or they can be cast on to the machine separately. The cast-on edge is usually neater than the cast-off edge and looks better as the outer edge of the collar.

A third method is to knit the collar vertically; it is knitted separately on a single- or double bed machine and attached later. Paper patterns are used to draft these collars; so for instance, flat collars can be drawn straight on to the neck edge of the body pattern and then traced off and adjusted. Alternatively, the neck measurements can be used to draft a variety of straight-edged collars. Shaping can be knitted into a basic collar, with partial knitting used to create darts around the neck (useful for an Eton collar style), or to add flare and create ruffles and frills.

2

Ruffled collar pattern

Ruffled collars are knitted on a single bed machine and can be attached to any type of neckline. They can vary in shape, fullness and depth. Multiples of lace knit can be layered to build large frilled collars.

1   On a piece of pattern paper draw a rectangle: the length should be the measurement of the neckline from centre front to centre back; the width should be the required depth of frill. This can be a shaped outside edge if you wish.
2   Divide the pattern into equal sections (see illustration 4). Open up these sections from the outside edge keeping the neck edge the original size (this will make a curved edge).
3   Keeping the paper pattern flat, draw around the new shape to include the opened sections. The wider these sections are, the fuller your frills will be. When you come to knit it, partial knitting can be used to shape the areas that are added.

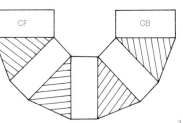

1   Collar design by Dulcie Wanless.
2   Large frilled collar by Juliana Sissons. Photography by Jojo Ma.
3   Illustration showing pattern cutting technique for frilled collar.

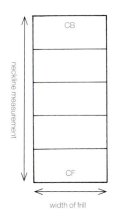

3

Collars and neckbands > Hems and edges

Hems and edges

1 Fancy hem, made using transfer stitch, by Zuzanna Fierro-Castro.
2 Detail of picot trim.
3 Detail of single bed mock rib.
4 Illustration showing double bed needle set-up.
5 Detail of double bed rib.

Hems and edges can be shaped, scalloped, fringed or laced. Hand-knitted trim can be transferred on to the needle bed to be knitted in and open stitches can be picked up from the machine to be continued on needles.

A normal cast-on edge will curl, but by hooking up the first row of knitting and knitting in with the body of the garment, you will create a far neater, tubular hem. The partial knitting technique also provides great possibilities for both hems and trims. A double bed machine can be used to produce a variety of ribbed edges. Mock ribs can be made on single beds; these are less elastic, but can give a good finish to a hem or cuff.

Weighted hems

Weights can be used in more formal knits to help the hang of a garment; they are usually enclosed inside the hem. There are many types, such as separate round or square lead weights, which are usually spaced out along the hem; weighted tapes, which have small lead pellets enclosed inside a cotton tube; various chain effects, which can be used as decorative weights; or ordinary self fabric/knit tape can be used to help give lightweight structure to a hem or edge.

1

Picot edge

1 Cast on in waste yarn, using a different colour to main knitting (this yarn will be unravelled and taken away later).
2 Change to main colour yarn and knit 10 rows.
3 Transfer every other stitch to adjacent needle (to form eyelets). Knit 10 rows.
4 Hook up the first row of loops from the main colour to form a hem. Knit as required.
5 Unravel the cast-on yarn. The trim will have a smoother join, without the cast-on edge.

2

Single bed mock rib (1x1)

1 Make the tension slightly tighter than the main knitting tension.
2 Cast on the needle selection with every other needle out of action.
3 Knit 10 rows. Knit 1 row on a slacker tension (for fold line). Knit 10 rows.
4 Hook up the first row of knitting on to the needles to form a hem.
5 Bring non-working needles forward to working position. Loosen the tension to the original main knitting tension. Knit as required.
6 A mock rib is quicker to do than a true rib (on a double bed machine) but it is not so elastic.

3

Basic double bed rib (1x1)

1 Set the needles as shown in the diagram; the needles out of action on one bed should be opposite the needles in working position on the other bed. Rack the beds so that the empty needles are lined up with the working needles on the opposite bed (on domestic machines, this is done by moving the pitch lever to P).
2 Take the carriage from left to right to form a zigzag row. Insert the cast on comb and wire.
3 Hang the weights on to the comb and set the cam levers to knit circular. Knitting alternate beds each row, knit 2 circular rows.
4 Reset the cam levers to knit normal (both beds together) and continue to knit.
5 If changing to all needles after the rib, rack the bed so that the needles being brought into action do not crash into working ones (H on a domestic machine).

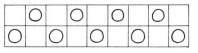

4

5

Collars and neckbands > **Hems and edges** > Buttonholes and fastenings

Scalloped hem

1. Thread up the machine with waste yarn and cast on 30 needles (each scallop will be 10 stitches wide).
2. Knit several rows in waste yarn and then 2 rows in the main yarn, ending with the carriage on the right-hand side.
3. Set holding cam levers to hold and bring 20 needles on the left to holding position. Knit 1 row.
4. Pull out the first right-hand needle to holding position and knit 1 row. Pull out the next needle on the left to holding position and knit 1 row. Continue to knit in this way, holding 1 needle after every row (alternating sides).
5. When only 1 needle is knitting, continue to knit by returning 1 needle after every row (alternating sides). When all needles are knitting again, stop and repeat this process on the middle 10 needles and then on the left 10 needles – when each scallop is being made, the other 2 scallops are on hold.
6. When all scallops have been made, take the holding cam levers off hold and knit 2 rows.
7. Pick up the first row in the main yarn and hook on to the needles to form a hem. Continue knitting.

1

Fringed trim

A braid with fringing can be knitted and then applied to the main body of a knitted piece at the edge or it can be hung on to the needles at any time during the knitting process.

1. Set the needles as for a large ladder, so for example, 5 needles in knitting position on either side of 40 out-of-action needles.
2. Cast on, leaving the 40 needles out of action between the two groups of needles in knitting position.
3. Knit the required amount of rows and cut through the middle of the floats to make two lengths of fringing.

1   Example of a scalloped hem on Victorian wool petticoat (hand-knitted).
2   Graph showing holding position on looped trim.
3   Pockets are a design feature of Hollie Maloney's work.
4   Pocket designs by Missoni A/W10. Catwalking.com.

Looped trim

1. This trim can be made by using the partial knitting technique. Thread up the machine and cast on 6 needles.
2. Knit 2 rows, finishing with the carriage on the right.
3. Set the holding cam levers to hold. Bring the first 2 needles on the left-hand side to holding position. Knit 8 rows.
4. Take the holding cam levers off hold and knit 2 rows.
5. Set the holding cam levers to hold. Repeat as before by holding the first 2 needles on the left for 8 rows before knitting 2 normal rows.
6. Continue in this way until the required length of braid has been knitted; the resulting braid will be looped. Explore this idea by varying the length and width of loops and by creating loops on either side of the central braid.

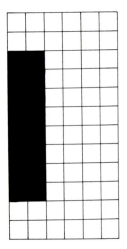

2

Pockets

There are three main styles of pocket, all of which are made in different ways. One style is the patch pocket, which is knitted separately (in any shape or size). Patch pockets are knitted upside down. A rib or hem edge is made first, for the pocket mouth. The rest of the patch is then knitted and sewn on by hand.

The second type is pockets made with horizontal slits. These have an opening in the main fabric and a pocket bag hanging inside. The pocket bag is most usually made in woven fabric.

The third type is the vertical slit pocket, which can be put in a side seam. If a pocket has a slanting top edge or a vertical opening, edging for the pocket mouth is knitted separately. Alternatively, the pocket may be knitted all in one with the garment using the partial knitting technique. The width of the pocket

is knitted whilst all other needles are held. The length of the pocket bag will need to be twice the depth measurement, so that it can be folded up to meet the pocket mouth. Knitting is then continued as normal and the sides of the pocket bag are hand-sewn later. The inside pocket bag could be knitted long enough for part of it to be pulled to the outside to form a flap.

3

4

Buttonholes and fastenings

1   Design by Simone Shailes, which
     features an unusual metal fastening.

There is a great variety of fastenings that can be used on knitwear and facings can be placed on knitted openings in much the same way as for openings on woven garments. For example, you could place a zip between the facing and the front edge or behind a knitted hem. Ties, cords, buttons, buckles and belts; hooks-and-eyes or fancy frogs and even crocheted bobbles and loops could all be considered as fastenings. Buttonholes, which could be the main design feature on a garment, can be made in a number of ways: horizontally or vertically, tiny or large. Vertical buttonholes are often made by partial knitting, whereas horizontal holes are made by casting off and casting on the required length (see the methods described on page 141). You could keep the buttonholes discreet or make a feature of them by embroidering with various stitches. You can also create buttonholes by leaving gaps when attaching a front band to a garment edge. More formal buttonholes may be made using the buttonhole attachment on a sewing machine.

1

Small buttonhole

1 Choose two adjacent needles.
2 Transfer 1 stitch to the left and 1 to the right. Knit 1 row.
3 Take the yarn out of the hooks of the two chosen needles and wind around each needle (as for an e-wrap cast-on).
4 Pull needles forward and knit 1 row. Pull needles forward and continue knitting.

Large buttonhole

1 Cast off the required amount of stitches using a contrast or same colour yarn.
  The ends of the cast-off yarn are left hanging either side of the buttonhole and will need to be sewn in later.
2 Cast on to the empty needles using the e-wrap method. Pull these needles fully forward and continue knitting.
3 Use a latch tool to neatly weave in the ends of yarn. A hand-sewn buttonhole stitch can be used to neaten the opening (see page 142).

Vertical buttonhole

1 Put the carriage to the right. Set the holding cam levers to hold.
2 Put all needles on the left of the buttonhole to holding position. Knit 6 rows.
3 Pull all the needles on the right of the buttonhole to holding position.
4 Break the yarn and take the carriage across to the left. Re-thread the yarn.
5 Push all needles on the left of the buttonhole back into working position with a latch tool. Knit 6 rows.
6 Pull all the needles on the left of the buttonhole to holding position.
7 Break the yarn and take carriage across to the right. Re-thread the yarn.
8 Take the holding cam levers off hold and continue to knit.

Rouleaux

Knitted rouleau loops can be used as button loops or can be pressed flat and used as an edging. The button loops can be set either individually or a whole row of loops can be made in a continuous strip and stitched between an outer edge and facing or sewn along a folded edge.

1   Cast on approximately 4 stitches.
2   Press one part button and knit as required. Alternatively, set all needles to slip when knitting every other row. If the tension is tight the cord will close to form a circular tube.

Buttonhole stitch

Buttonhole stitch is used to strengthen a button loop (which should be large enough for the button to go through). Contrasting or matching threads can be used, as can decorative cords and narrow braids.

1   Take a length of sewing thread and stitch an arch with a loop of the thread.
2   Starting on the left, thread the needle in and behind the arch of the thread, but in front of the new loop being formed with the stitch.
3   Continue making stitches tightly together, until the arch is covered, then secure the last stitch with a knot.

1

2

Buttons

Buttons can be modern, plastic, glass or vintage, they can be covered in contrast fabrics or fine knits; they can be bobbles or toggles or made from crochet. Whichever you choose, the garment should be finished and steamed before the buttons are sewn on. If the button is for decoration only, it can be sewn flat against the knit; otherwise it will need a stem.

Sewing on a button

The length of the stem should allow the button to sit in the buttonhole comfortably but it should not be so long that the button flops to one side when not buttoned up.

1 Hold the button just above the surface of the knit to make the stem.
2 Make approximately 6 stitches through the holes of the button, holding the button and adjusting the stitches to make them the same length.
3 Sew a buttonhole stitch around the group of threads, from the button down to the base of the stem.
4 Finish with several small stitches to fasten the thread.

3

1   Rouleau loop braid on Victorian wool jacket.
2   Illustration showing buttonhole stitch.
3   Selection of buttons photographed by Jojo Ma.

Hems and edges > **Buttonholes and fastenings** > Hand-finishing techniques

Hand-finishing techniques

1   Knit by Dulcie Wanless.
2–3 Bocked and pressed samples by
      Annabel Scopes. These were made
      on a Dubied machine with alternative
      needles transferred to the back bed
      and then mattress-stitched together.

Making up a garment is one of the most important parts of production. The knitted pieces may look even, but incorrect blocking, pressing and making-up can ruin an otherwise well-knitted garment.

When knitting a long length of fabric it is a good idea to put yarn markers along the edges of the knit, at regular intervals – for example, every 100 rows or so. These can be matched at the making-up stage to keep the edges straight and in line. The knitted fabric tends to be very stretched when it first comes off the machine so it is important to block out the size and press each garment piece before making up.

1

In the industry

Over the following pages there are a series of mini-case studies and interviews with a range of knit designers and specialists. These serve to illustrate the different ways you can work with knitted textiles, offering inspiration and insight into the range of careers within the knitwear industry.

Malcolm McInnes designs for his own menswear label: casual luxury sportswear, with a strong, cutting-edge design element. He is also Head of Fashion at Brighton University.

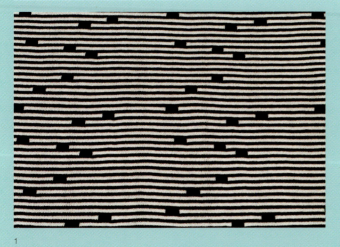

1

What is your design background and why did you go into knitwear?
I studied Fashion and Textiles at Central St Martins and had almost an obsessive love for working with the fine-gauge knitting machines and handling silk and viscose yarns.

I have always been careful to be labelled as a knitwear designer. Shape, overall silhouette and concept are my first considerations in designing for the fashion market. My particular focus in knitwear is the use of contrasting colour and patterning techniques. One might argue why knitting, if you can achieve the same through printed fabrics? I find that natural cashmere and silk yarns take colour beautifully, and this can be exciting to work with, in achieving new colour languages, particularly for menswear.

Can you talk us through your design process?
Almost always the use of saturated pure colour drives the development of the collection, together with the use of primary geometric structures that translate surface patterning in some form across the piece. I first plot how best to balance and distribute the chosen colours for the season in the range of garments I intend to produce; I group then by themes. I then evolve the simple geometric shapes into pattern compositions to achieve quite flat surface qualities and then concentrate on cut, fashioning and finishing detail, to achieve the sophisticated and restraining aesthetic I constantly look for.

At the end of each sales season I evaluate with my team what has been the most successful in the collection and what has not. This evaluation may determine to some extent the product development for the following season. One advantage I do have is the menswear collection is small and is aimed at a niche market; there is little need to follow the trends set by prediction companies.

I spend a lot of time testing the decorative ideas for the fabrics and the distribution of them over the knitted pieces, gauging constantly how they would sit on the body and whether my client would wear them. I am conscious of final fabric weights and tend to work with 12-gauge and 7-gauge solutions. I may have one or two pieces that are heavier each season in the collection. These garments are normally designed for the purposes of editorial, and not for selling.

What advice could you give to graduates starting out in the industry?
If I had any advice for someone wanting to work in menswear as a designer, and specifically knitwear, I would say passion is the most important ingredient. Take any experience that comes your way, as in time you will understand the significance of this. All opportunities you can learn and grow from. Even if you start with a humble job in a large design company, apart from your own duties, you are able to observe those of others in the company and gain a greater knowledge of the processes and procedures in building such a large-scale enterprise.

1   Fringes.
2   Finishing stitch.
3   Picot edge stitch.
4   Backstitch.
5   Three-bead back stitch.
6   Parallel stitch.
7   Couching stitch.
8   Running stitch.
9   Selection of swatches with vintage beads, by Rebecca Mears.

9

Hand-finishing techniques > **Embellishment** > In the industry

Beading

Beading is another form of embroidery, which may be used to cover the whole of the knitted piece or to decorate edges, trims and motifs. Beads may be attached at the knitting stage, by weaving in beaded lengths of thread, or else by threading on to the stitch with a special tool.

Beaded embellishments can be worked with gold or silver thread, using a variety of beads, from cultured pearls to steel, glass and wood. Lengths of sequins and fancy braids may also be attached in similar ways. The process is time-consuming, which adds considerable cost to the end design.

If sewing beads on to the knit you will need to use a sewing needle that is large enough for the thread to fit through the eye but small enough to go through the hole in the bead. There are various different stitching methods, such as backstitch, parallel stitch, couching stitch and running stitch, as shown in the illustrations on the right. In specialist workrooms a tambour hook is usually used for beading. This tool is similar to a crochet hook and it is used to attach strings of beads with chain stitch. This method allows for finer work with small beads: the tambour hook makes chain stitches around the thread holding the beads and, as such, does not need to fit through the beads. However, if the thread breaks, the beads will soon fall off. Beads that are individually sewn with a needle are more secure (although this is, of course, very time-consuming).

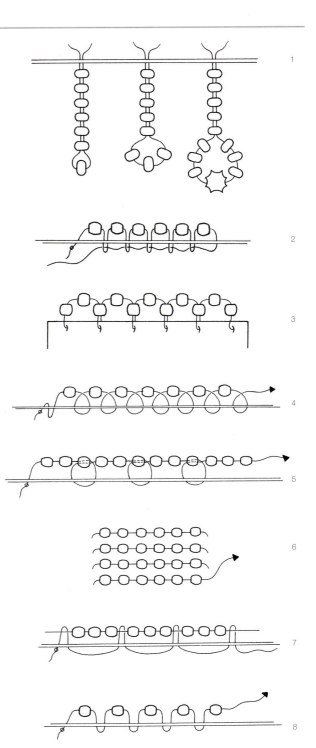

1

2

3

4

5

6

7

8

3

4

Simple stitches

A line of stitches with a coloured thread on a contrast background fabric is a simple form of decoration in itself. There are a variety of simple, well-known stitches, which form the basis of more advanced embroidery design, if required.

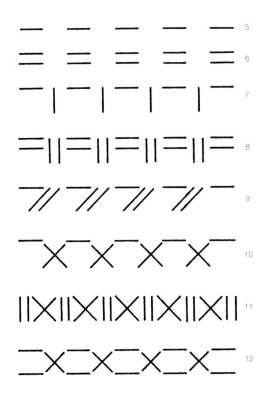

5

6

7

8

9

10

11

12

1. 1950s cream lambswool and pearl button cardigan with ribbon and silk thread floral embroidery.
2. Selection of machine-embroidered trims.
3–4 Hand-embroidered knitted swatches by Zuzana Fierro-Castro.
5. Running stitch.
6. Double tracking.
7. Upright row of stitches between running stitch.
8. Double rows.
9. Slanting stitch.
10. Cross stitch with running stitch.
11. Vertical upright stitches with cross stitch.
12. Combination of cross stitch and tacking stitch.

1

Embroidery

The art of embroidery can add colour and durability to a knitted garment. Stitches can be used to transform plain knits into creative pieces of art. Decorative stitches can be made in silk, wool, linen threads or with unusual materials such as leather and ribbons. Consider colour proportion and weight of yarn along with texture, stitches, lines and masses. Many rich or light and dainty designs in embroidery can be produced.

When designing for embroidery it is better to keep the shapes simple because of the intricacy of the pattern formed by the stitches. In many instances, it is possible to produce good embroidery design without drawing first. The simplest form of design is based on repetition, when stitches are placed together to form decorative borders.

Appliqué

Appliqué is one of the most versatile embellishments, formed by applying decorative fabrics to the surface of the main fabric. These can be contrasting silks, cottons, linens or leather, they can be knitted, woven or felted shapes, cut or fully-fashioned. Appliquéd fabrics can be hemmed and hand-sewn or left raw-edged and embroidered. For thicker materials, such as leather, it is easier to punch holes through the edges and embroider them on to the garment. Larger motifs are easier to sew if they are basted on to the garment with large tacking threads, to keep them in place whilst sewing. Bear in mind that non-stretch appliqué fabrics will restrict the stretch of the garment.

1   Two-tone chocolate knit, with hand-knotted lace medallion embellishment, by Amy Phipps.

Embellishment

Embroidery, appliqué and beading are all forms of embellishment often used on couture garments, whether they are woven or knitted. Knitted swatch makers often employ a dedicated embellisher, whose job is to embroider or bead swatches before they are put on headers, ready to be sold. There are specialised embroidery firms that offer a variety of embellishment services.

Consider the scale and size of the garment before designing any embellishments. Paper patterns can be made to check the size of a motif. Embroidery frames are helpful for appliqué, embroidery and beading because they hold the fabric tight, making it easier to work with. Most embellishments are worked from the right side of the fabric, apart from some beading techniques, which are worked from the wrong side.

Hemming stitch

Hemming stitch can be used to attach top edges, bands and hems. If sewing open edges, remember to sew each stitch separately.

1. Turn the hem or collar and baste or pin in place.
2. Starting on the right, push the needle into the first open stitch and up through the corresponding stitch of the main knitting. The stitch should be invisible from the right side.

Grafting

Grafting is used to join two sections of knit together to give the appearance of a continuous piece of knitting. The knitted stitches are held on waste yarn, which is unravelled during the grafting procedure. If done neatly it is an invisible join, because it imitates a row of knitting.

1. Hold the two pieces of knitting edge to edge and face up. Start from the right side.
2. Push the needle through the first and second stitches on the top edge, through the first and second stitches on the bottom edge, then through the second and the third stitches on the top edge and continue along the row.
3. Do not pull the sewn stitches any tighter than the knitted stitches.

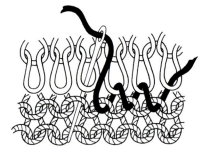

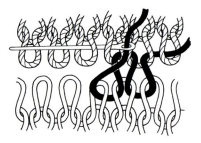

Waste yarn is also used when a piece of knitting needs to be returned to the needles on the machine, at a later stage. The waste yarn is unravelled to the last row and then unravelled a stitch at a time whilst the main knitting is placed back on to the needles with a transfer tool. Alternatively, the main colour stitches can be picked up whilst the waste is still attached (either above the bed or tucked below) and then unravelled before knitting starts.

Waste knitting can also be used for shaping. If part of a garment is cast on or finished off in waste, it can be temporarily taken off the machine to allow the remainder to be shaped.

Mattress stitch

Mattress stitch is used to make an invisible join and for when a strong seam is required, without bulk. It is worked from the right side, making it a useful stitch for matching patterns and stripes.

1　Hold the two pieces edge to edge and work from right to left. Pass the needle under two bars, one stitch in from the edge, on both pieces.
2　Continue stitching; after every few stitches gently pull the thread to close the seam.
3　Finish with the end of the thread down the inside of the seam.

Backstitch

Backstitch can be used to sew an open edge on to a closed edge. It is useful for casting off ribs and can be used for seams without stretch.

1　Overlap the two pieces by one or two rows.
2　Push the needle into the first stitch, through the under layer and then up through the second stitch.
3　Take the needle back into the first stitch and under layer again and up through the third stitch, then back into the second stitch and up through the fourth. Repeat along the row of stitches.

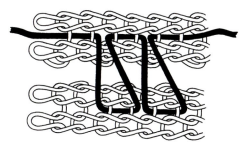

Waste knitting techniques
There are various useful techniques that involve knitting in waste yarn. If two edges are to be joined by grafting, the edges need to have open stitches. Waste yarn is knitted on to the row of the main knitting instead of casting off in the normal way, which holds the stitches together until the grafting process; the waste yarn is unravelled during this process or at the end.

2

Linkers
Linkers

Linkers are used to join knitted fabrics together. Smaller versions of industrial linkers are available, which are either electronic or hand-operated. A linker allows any length of knitting to be joined, because the work is pushed on to a ring of circular needles, right sides together. As the machine is operated, a chain-stitch is formed, joining the two fabrics together. After the first part of the work is linked it can be removed, to make room for the other end of the knitting to be placed on the needles.

Blocking and pressing

Blocking involves pinning out the garment pieces to the required shape and measurements and then steaming them. It is possible to pin the knit over the paper pattern, but this may ruin the paper, which would make it difficult to reuse. Another method of blocking is to mark the pattern shape on to a cotton calico fabric and pin the knitted piece over that.

When steaming, gently move the iron above the surface and release the steam (do not press down on the fabric at all). Let the fabric rest on a flat surface (a blocking board) to set. Special care should be applied to the edges as some yarns curl more than others. Wool and natural fibres can be steamed or, if you do not have a steam iron, cover the knit with a damp cloth. Ribs can be steamed if they are made of natural fibres, but keep them closed up: if they are steamed when extended they will stay extended. Synthetic fibres should not be steamed at all because it makes them less elastic. It is possible to iron the fabric from the wrong side, with no pressure applied.

Seams

Seams on knitted garments should be invisible; they should be sewn together using a similar tension to the pieces that are being joined. If the seam is sewn too tight it will gather and the stitches will break; if too loose, it will gape and the stitches will be visible.

Knitted pieces can be sewn together by hand, with a sewing machine or by using a linker (see right). For hand-sewing, use a blunt knitwear needle with a thinner version of the main thread. If the knitting yarn is textured, a matching plain yarn can be used. Fine or weak yarns will need to be doubled.

Sewing machines

Making up on a sewing machine is a very quick and efficient way of stitching garment pieces together. Many mass-produced garments are made from a cut-and-sew method and the edges overlocked to stop the knit from unravelling. Some makes of machine have a special stitch foot for sewing up knitwear. It is a good idea to baste the edges of the garment pieces together and use a polyester thread in the machine and bobbin case.

If you desire to set up your own brand or work freelance for other companies, you must be knowledgeable of the business element to the discipline too. This is important when negotiating business contracts and arrangements. It is rare that one is able to be creative and business-minded with the same measure of success. So what is important is that you surround yourself with trusted and able business partners to take care of this aspect of the work.

2

1–2   Computer-generated 12-gauge circular knitting in geometric pattern by Malcolm McInnes.

3   The Perfect, 2007. Installation of machine-knitted wool, using a Shima Seiki WholeGarment®, at Vestlandske Kunstindustrimuseum, Bergen, Norway.

Freddie Robins, London-based textile artist

Freddie Robins was taught to knit at a young age and she fell in love with it. When she was 17 she entered a knitwear design competition in a national craft magazine and, after winning, went on to study knitted textiles at both Middlesex Polytechnic (now Middlesex University) and the Royal College of Art in London. She has been working as an artist using knitted textiles as her primary medium since 1997.

A recent body of work, The Perfect, deals with the constant drive for perfection. It is made using technology developed for mass production, to make garment multiples that are exactly the same as each other: garments that do not require any hand finishing, garments whose manufacture does not produce any waste, garments whose production does not require the human touch. Garments that are, in fact, perfect.

She produced these knitted multiples through the use of a Shima Seiki WholeGarment® machine. These multiples take the form of life size, three-dimensional human bodies. She has combined them in a variety of different ways to create large-scale knitted sculptures and installations.

3

Embellishment > In the industry

Shelley Fox is known for her conceptual, directional work. She designed for her own label between 1996 and 2006, producing seasonal collections and collaborating with practitioners outside the fashion industry. She is now Donna Karan Professor of Fashion Design at Parsons, New York.

What is your design background and why did you want to become a designer?

I graduated from Central St Martins, with a BA in textiles, and then after six months of working for designer Joe Casely-Hayford, went on to do an MA in fashion at St Martins. I swung towards knit because I wanted to develop fabrics, to see where they went. But I was also interested in patterns and woven fabrics.

You are known for your experimental approach to fabric treatments. How would you describe your signature work?

Felting has always been a big part of my collections. In my BA, the felting came about because the fine-gauge machines were always broken. I would spend ages trying to make a fine-knit dress on the knitting machine, and then it would always muck up at the last minute, so I felted out the mistakes. I created scorching effects by leaving the fabric too long in the heat press – a further development in the design process. This was my introduction to felt and heat transfer. Then, when my fabrics happened, I could see my collection coming together. An integral part of my design process was working in 3D and building with fabric.

1–2   For this collection, blow-torched sequins and cascading felt frills were combined with geometric cutting techniques. The felt frills were handmade, becoming the main part of the fabric; almost coming out of the fabric. A/W00. Photography by Chris Moore.

How does your work take new direction and what are your inspirations?

Elastoplast finger plasters and bandages were the source materials for my A/W97 collection: intrigued by the plasters I had for a cut on my leg, I came up with the idea of using plasters and bandaging fabrics. I contacted a pharmaceutical company Smith & Nephew, who sent me their fabric archive, and I began to use Elastoplast fabric. The collection featured felted wools. I put too much in the washing machine and it came out scarred and rippled. It was another accident, but once I had printed on it, it became the signature for the collection. The ripples and scars were a happy accident, in turn a further development on the medical theme. My main inspirations are history, Morse code and Braille in cloth. The Morse code was the starting position, it developed into sound for the show and visual for the cloth. Words such as cocoon, wrap or layer can be used to sustain a whole project and trigger interesting starting points for development. For my Autumn/Winter 2001 collection I used my diaries as inspiration. The diary print was taken from a series of business diaries; certain pages were selected based on their composition and assembled to make a print. The collection was a mixture of evening sweat shirting, cashmere, diary scribble graphic prints and oversized cable knitwear. The colours were a natural palette of black, putty and highlights of mint green, bright reds and primrose yellows. In my A/W98 collection, I used the concept of Braille: the simplicity of the alphabet shapes and codes. It was the method of touch reading that inspired my development into the use of Braille markings on wool (felted knit). This fabric was then transformed into three-dimensional geometric shapes, which were drafted on the body.

Research and development is an integral part of your work and you have recently been working on a Nobel textiles project, in collaboration with the Medical Research Council; could you tell us more?

For this we worked with MRI scanners to study body shapes. Medical research was carried out on six female volunteers, who were scanned and tagged, to make sure they went to the gym! I used my body as an example and ran the New York Marathon to record body change. We also looked at vintage clothing, dressmaking patterns that had been passed down through families, to explore the body changes and the clothing changes in parallel. Vintage clothing was unpicked and restructured. The group project was a Central St Martins/ICA collaboration of textile designers and scientists.

You have collaborated with many artists; how does working on your label differ creatively from working with people such as the dancer, Michael Clark?

You are working for someone else's final product so you have to take on board their vision. When working with Random Dance, I was dealing with dancers. The body requirements are different, and I had to think of the practicalities, such as sweat, so I had to think in a different way. When working on school uniforms, I am working with narrow parameters, which help you focus in a different way, but are still stimulating.

2

3

3 Collection 15, Reissue, was developed from favourite patterns in the Shelley Fox pattern archive. Diary print was produced in a varied colour palette and sweatshirting was mixed with a smashed glass beaded fabric. A/W03. Photography by Wilson Kao.

Embellishment > In the industry

Sue Enticknap is design director of Knit-1, which specialises in selling one-off copyright designs to the worldwide fashion industry.

What is a typical day for you?

Today was fairly typical: in at around 8am. Check the progress of the previous day's designs. Design/sketch/selection process for today's prints. Check progress of any sewing. Start to make a knitwear design. Check emails. Answer the phone. Check the studio is not running out of cloth/printing media/thread/coffee etc. Photograph any finished designs. Discuss and book selling trips. Machine maintenance. Check on schedule of visiting Indian beading supplier. Check visit of Topshop buyer. Review designs in current collection due to be sold in New York in two weeks' time.

How do you begin the design approach? Is it with the knitted fabric or the construction?

I have studied fashion and the fashion cycle for over 30 years. If you observe carefully you can predict trends quite easily as a lot of fashion looks backwards. I begin to design by developing an idea about technique or silhouette. I consider my work to be a continuous process – it doesn't 'stop and start'.

I work on the knit machine and start creating the fabric into a garment. Because we only make one-offs this can be very creative and it doesn't have to be repeated: no pattern is made. The piece will be stitched together; it may be finished in the washing machine or hand-washed and steamed. It is then given a reference number and photographed for our records.

How important is research in the design process? Where do you get your inspiration from?

Research is very important. Inspiration can come from fashion, antique textiles, nature, artists or something completely random. My brain never turns off from possible ideas, so it can be anything. I made a design the other day from something I saw in the dentist's waiting room and I drew an idea on the back of an envelope.

1

Where/how do you sell your knitted swatches?

We sell at trade shows in Europe and the US and also by visiting our customers at their offices throughout the world.

Do factors such as sales figures impact upon your design decisions?

If you don't respect sales you won't have a business!

Do you design for a specific customer in mind? What kind of customer wears your designs?

Yes, every time I make/design something I have a customer profile in mind. If I had a design but couldn't think who would wear it then I would consider that design to have failed and it would not be put into our collection. We sell to all levels/ages/profiles of the market, from babies to grannies and everyone in between.

Do you work to a brief?

Yes, especially in connection with seasons. We can't sell designs out of season. Also, fabric, colour, pattern and silhouette are very important.

How do you promote your designs?

By visiting our customers regularly.

How much time do you spend on construction?

Each design takes a maximum of one day to make from start to finish.

What is your favourite aspect of the job?

Designing on the dummy.

And your least favourite?

Government bureaucracy. Dealing with tax, VAT, accounts, health and safety, insurance....

What advice can you give to aspiring knitwear designers?

This industry is extremely competitive. Be the best.

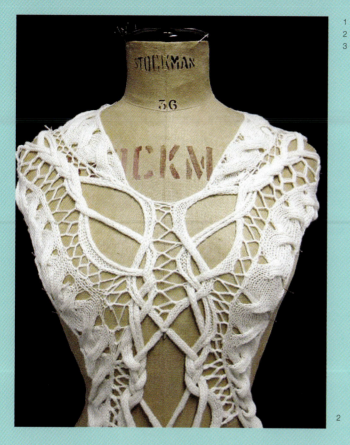

1 Knit-1 pointelle design.
2 Knit-1 cable design.
3 This knitted tube worn on the upper
body has a series of holes that can
be used as arm or neck holes as the
wearer wishes. Holes that are not
used can be left unopened by leaving
the drawthread embedded in the
knitted textile. Photography by Moose
Azim. Model Laura Higgs.

2

Caterina Radvan, knitwear designer and PhD researcher at London College of Fashion

Caterina Radvan's research seeks
to identify disabled women's
requirements of fashion and to
establish criteria for the design of a
set of knitwear prototypes, which
will inform the design of a collection
of knitwear through advanced
knitting technology. Fashion today
is designed with only non-disabled
women in mind, which means
disabled women are denied access
to wearable fashion and to the same
benefits of clothing and fashion that
non-disabled women enjoy.

Her method of design development
has followed an empirical approach
to garment shape, based on the
avoidance of traditional pattern
cutting blocks. Instead, basic
geometric shapes are used as a
starting point; and instead of using
traditional darting techniques to
resolve the problem of fit, it was
decided to exaggerate the problem
by adding extra fabric so that the
resulting folds and waves of fabric
become the feature of the design.
The medium of seamless knitting
is incorporated into the inclusive
design principle.

3

Embellishment > In the industry

1   Architectural knit design *Slow Furl*. Knitted textiles were used as part of an architecture exhibition by Mette Ramsgard Thomsen and Karin Bech. This naturally pliable knitted textile was slowly moved around by the use of robotic structures hidden behind a wall.

The aim of this book has to been to offer inspiration and insight into the different elements of knitwear design and to introduce you to as many basic machine techniques as possible. I hope that the knitting techniques have inspired you to play with yarns, scale and different sequences. Remember, only a few techniques need to be mastered at the beginning – one technique can be used in numerous ways.

The opportunities for design within the knit industry are broad and diverse. A designer may pursue a career within a large company, or as a designer/maker in a small business, taking advantage of knit's unique bespoke factor. Some designers work for swatch studios, creating knit concepts to be sold to the fashion/interior design industry. Other knitwear graduates go on to work in trend forecasting, styling and costume design. Those with more technical expertise may work as consultants on collaborative projects within medical textiles, geo-textiles and architecture. Recently, there has been significant interest in fashion and well being. Researcher Vikki Haffenden, for example, has applied knit technology to large-size women's body shapes; with the use of three-dimensional body scans and specialist software she has developed better-fit knitwear for the larger lady (Knit to Fit). The career opportunities are hugely varied, so take time to consider the ways in which you can take your knitwear design when you finish your course.

It is hoped that the contents of this book will encourage you to become more curious about different aspects of knit and to start your own investigations. Remember to learn the basics first and then start experimenting. Hopefully this book will help you feel confident in making your own patterns and further your interests in knitted textiles and fashion.

Acetate
Semi-synthetic yarn made from cellulose pulp and acetic acid.

Acrylic
Synthetic version of wool, developed by DuPont in the 1940s.

Agent
Person authorised to act on your behalf to sell your garments.

Alpaca
Soft, fine hair from the alpaca goat.

Appliqué
Fabric, beads or stitches sewn on to a fabric/knit as embellishment.

Angora
Fine, light hair combed from the angora rabbit.

Aran
A textured knit that incorporates cables, made using transfer tools.

Asymmetrical
A garment that has two different sides.

Beaded knitting
The beads are threaded on to the yarn; they can then knitted into the work using the knit weave method.

Bind off
The technique of finishing and taking the knit off the machine (cast off).

Block
Primary pattern used as starting point for garment patterns.

Bodice
The upper body of a garment.

Bouclé
Fancy yarn containing loops.

Brief
Set of instructions directed at a designer to outline project aims, objectives and final outcomes.

Cable stitch
The crossings of groups of stitches, repeated at intervals in the same wales (ornamental twisting of wales).

Cam
Part of the mechanics found under the carriage of a knitting machine; when put in position, these determine the needle movement and therefore the stitch effect.

Carriage
The principal part of a knitting machine, it carries the cams across the bed.

Cashmere
Hair from the fine, soft undercoat of the cashmere goat; a luxury yarn.

Cast on
Various ways of initiating stitches on empty needles.

Chainette
Fancy yarn consisting of chain-looped stitches or a tube of stitches.

Chart
A knitted pattern plotted on graph paper.

Chenille
Fancy yarn with a velvet-like texture.

Computer Aided Design (CAD)
The use of computers in fashion and knitwear design.

Conceptual
A design vision based on ideas and principles.

Cone
Support for yarn.

Cord
Small tube of knitting.

Cottage industry
The garments are usually produced in the home of the maker.

Cotton
Fibre from the cotton plant. Versatile and soft.

Crepe
Yarn or fabric with a crinkled texture, often with an element of stretch.

Dart
Shaped area of knit, tapered at one end or both ends to enable a better fit.

Decrease
Way of reducing the width of fabric by knitting two or more stitches together.

Design swatch
Finished design for sale through an agent.

Double bed
Knitting machines that have two beds, hence two rows of needles facing each other.

Double jersey
Plain, double-faced, reversible knit, made on a double bed machine. Ideal for jackets and heavier garments.

Drape
The way a fabric hangs.

Embellishment
Decoration stitched or appliquéd on to a fabric/knit.

Embroidery
Decorative stitches sewn on to knit as an embellishment.

Eyelet
A hole formed by transferring a stitch and leaving the empty needle in action, so that it casts on in the next row knitted (one of the basic techniques for lace knitting).

Face / right side
The most interesting side of a fabric/knit.

Fair Isle
A single jersey knit with small patterns using two colours at a time; creates floats at the back of the fabric.

Fashion forecasting
The process of predicting forthcoming trends.

Felt
A thick fabric made from wool. The fibres are matted and fused together during a process involving water and heat. There is no grain to these fabrics and they are ideal for cutting as they do not unravel.

Float
Threads that pass the needles and are not knitted in.

Fully fashioned
The shaping of a knitwear garment so each edge has a wale travelling along the line of the selvedge.

Garter stitch
Alternate rows of knit and purl.

Gauge
The number of needles in one inch of the bed. The resulting fabric is knitted in a certain gauge, depending on the size of the machine.

Gimp
Fancy yarn with a wavy structure.

Grafting
A sewing technique that creates an invisible join.

Guernsey/gansey
A traditional fisherman's jumper.

Hank/skein
Quantity of yarn that has not been wound on to a cone.

Haute couture
Exclusive garments individually designed for private clients.

High end
Expensive garments, below haute couture, usually produced in limited numbers.

Holding stitches
Stitches that are held on non-knitting needles over a series of courses when other needles are knitting.

Increase
Methods for increasing the width of the knit by adding new stitches.

Inlay
Technique for holding an inlay yarn in place between or over the needles; it is then woven in when knitted.

Intarsia
A method of knitting single, non-repeating motifs or large areas of contrasting colour. A more time-consuming technique than Fair Isle and jacquard.

Jacquard
A double jersey knit using a punch card or electronic machine to create a pattern. This technique allows the floats to be knitted in at the back.

Knit pattern
Instructions for knitting up a garment; it will indicate how many stitches and rows to knit for each section of the silhouette, as well as the gauge, yarn and stitch types to use.

Knitted lace
A single jersey fabric with eyelet hole patterns; made with a lace carriage or by hand-tooling techniques.

Knit weave
This involves placing a thick yarn across a fine one while it is knitted. The thick yarn is then knitted in with the fine knitting, giving one side of the work a woven appearance.

Knop
Fancy yarn with small lumps along its length.

Lace
Fabric with transparent and opaque areas, which can be made using a lace carriage or transfer tools.

Ladders
Technique in which stitches are dropped and left to unravel, this can be achieved accidentally or by design.

Lambswool
100% virgin wool.

Latch up
The use of a latch tool to reform dropped stitches or to pick up floats of a ladder.

Linen
Fibre from the flax plant.

Lurex
Fancy yarn made from laminate or plasticized metal.

Lycra
Synthetic elastic fibre, developed by DuPont.

Market
The business or trade of a particular type of product.

Marl/twist yarn
Yarn made from two or more yarns twisted together.

Mass-market fashion
Ready-to-wear clothes produced in large quantities and standard sizes.

Merino
High-quality wool from the merino sheep.

Mohair
Yarn made from the hair of the angora goat.

Moss stitch
Technique of single plain and purl stitches that alternate both vertically and horizontally.

Niche
Specialised product group targeting a specific area of the market.

Nylon
Synthetic, polyamide yarn.

Partial row knitting (holding technique)
Working with part of a row at one time. Over a series of rows, the knitter can decrease the number of stitches to create a three-dimensional texture or shaped blocks of colour.

Pattern pieces
Paper templates used to inform the silhouette of a garment; these shapes can be the starting points for creating knit patterns (see knit pattern).

Picot hem
A lace-patterned hem made with eyelet holes.

Plating
The knitting of two yarns simultaneously; when knitting a single jersey, one yarn is visible on the face and the other on the reverse; when knitting a double jersey the second yarn is hidden in the centre of the knit and is only revealed when stitches are taken out of action to show the interior.

Glossary

Racking
Technique used when knitting on two beds; one needle bed can be moved, so that it is not lined up with the other, crossing stitches over each other in a lateral direction.

Rayon
Regenerated cellulose yarn made from wood pulp.

Rib
Wales of plain and purl stitches forming a stretchy fabric. Ideal for trims on garments at the waist, neck or wrists.

Row count
The number of passes of the carriage as counted by the row counter on the machine.

Sample swatch
First versions of a design to trial technique and colour.

Selvedge
Closed side edges of the knit.

Short row
Technique for changing direction of knitting before the end of a row.

Silhouette
The outline shape of a garment or collection.

Single jersey
A lightweight fabric made on a single bed machine. Ideal for T-shirts and lingerie.

Sinker gate
A row of pins along the front of the needle bed.

Stand
A dress-making mannequin or dummy; also known as form.

Stitch
A single loop of yarn within the knit.

Target market
The group of customers that a retailer aims to sell to.

Tension swatch
A knitted swatch used to calculate stitches and rows for knitting final designs.

Toile
First version of a garment in cheap fabric.

Transfer stitch
Moving a stitch loop to a nearby needle.

Tuck stitch
The yarn is collected and held on a needle without being knitted in.

Wale
Column of knit stitches.

Warp knitting
Consists of vertical chains of loops; these loops connect with each other across the entire width of the knit. Ideal for summer wear, sports wear and lingerie.

Waste knitting
Knitting worked with waste or scrap yarn; when casting on it provides an area of knit to hang weights on and can act as a stitch holder for knitting that needs to be put back on to the needles.

Weft knitting
Consists of a succession of loops repeated across the width of the knitting, one row of loops connects with the next row of loops forming a length of knit.

Woollen-spun yarn
Yarn that is soft, bulky and light, which has been spun from fibres that have been carded, but not combed. Does not necessarily have to contain wool.

Worsted
Tightly spun, smooth wool yarn. The fibres are combed parallel, which makes the yarn smooth and strong.

Yarn count
Information on the thickness of yarn, in relation to the length and weight. There are a number of systems: in the metric system, the finer the yarn, the higher the number; for example, 2/32s is finer than 2/28s.

Reading basic symbols

Symbols and charts are the easiest way to explain step-by-step instructions for a knitting technique. Simple machine knitting charts are usually written to show the reverse face side of the fabric, as the knitter would see it hanging off the machine. More complex, fashioned charts may be written to be read from the front and will not have the purl symbols. This is because in fashioned work it is necessary to indicate the final sloping direction of the stitches.

A diagram will illustrate the needle set-up and it should indicate which stitches to move, which direction to move them in and how many stitches to transfer in one move. It will also indicate how many rows to knit. The symbols shown here are for simple charts.

Lifted stitch. An arrow indicates where to lift and hang a stitch. The base of the arrow shows the stitch being lifted and the point of the arrow shows the needle and row on which the stitch is being hung.

Purl or reverse stitch. When work is hung on the machine, this is the side that faces the knitter.

Tuck stitch. Alternating pattern produced by tucking every other needle. This pattern can be knitted by selecting the tucking cams on the carriage or by using holding position to accumulate tucks.

Slip stitch. This shows on the purl side of the fabric; it can be formed by selecting slip stitch on the carriage or can be formed manually.

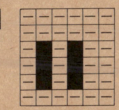

Holding position. This sample shows needles 2 and 4 being held. Tuck stitches are formed over rows 2, 3 and 4.

Holding position. Needles are held to form short rows. The holding needles are gradually increased with each row.

Domestic knitting machines

Knitmaster

Knitmaster machines are no longer in production but second-hand machines are available. These are good, basic single bed machines that include a punch card mechanism and can be adapted into double bed machines with the addition of a ribber. Lace carriages, intarsia carriages and weave attachments can also be bought separately for this make of machine. Fine gauge machines are rare and therefore more expensive. Knitmaster chunky gauge machines, which have punch cards, are good for beginners but are limited on patterning.

Silver Reed

These machines are of the same design as the now discontinued Knitmaster, but offer a more modern selection of machines. There are electronic versions of all three gauges, but they are expensive and require their own electronic programming system. Punch card versions of the standard gauge are still available new. The Knitmaster brand of colour changers fit on to all of the Knitmaster and Silver Reed machines. The YC6 is best because it converts from a single to a double bed. Some more recent Knitmaster ribbers fit Silver Reed machines.

Brother

Another popular brand of domestic knitting machine (formerly called Jones Brother). These are no longer available to buy new in the UK. These machines differ from the Knitmaster in patterning mechanisms but otherwise are very much the same. Some of the older Brother machines do not come with lace carriages and some of the older chunky gauge machines do not have punch card mechanisms but are still good for manually manipulated chunky cables. If buying an electronic Brother machine, the 950 or 950i models onwards are the best; older ones should be avoided unless seen working (although these should be cheap to buy). The 950 is an old electronic machine but is good to use if you have a healthy supply of Mylar sheets to work with. The 950i has a larger patterning mechanism and has the capacity to download patterns from a PC computer with the DesignaKnit package. The Brother 965 and 965i models are similar to the 950 and 950i versions, but are newer and have a slightly different programming system. All need special leads to download patterns from a PC. Not all Brother ribbers fit the electronic machines. Brother colour changers do fit all machines and there are two colour changers: one single bed and one double bed.

Passap

This is the most well-known make of domestic double bed machine. They are similar to an industrial Dubied, in that they have a permanent double bed. They are no longer available new. Attachments can be added to the basic model to make up a more advanced version or advanced versions can be purchased complete with a four-colour changer and an automatic punch card pattern unit and motor. Electronic versions E6000 and E8000 were made of this machine and the later models can be used with DesignaKnit software, again with the special cable connection.

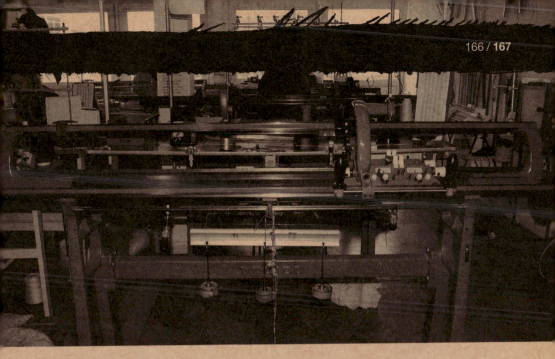

Yarn counts

Yarn counts are systems that indicate the thickness and relative weight of yarn. These systems can provide a way of working out the length of yarn needed. A traditional system uses two figures, such as 2/6s (pronounced two sixes). The first figure relates to how many single ply/strands make up the yarn. The second figure points to the weight of each single strand. In most traditional systems, it refers to the number of hanks to the pound of yarn. The higher the number of hanks to the pound, the thinner the yarn is likely to be.

In order to work out the length and weight of yarn required, you would first need to know the standard length of yarn in a hank. This will vary, depending on the type of yarn. For cotton, the standard length is 840 yards. For worsted wool it is 560 yards.

If, for example, you wanted to use a worsted wool yarn at 560 yards per hank, which is labelled 2/6s, you would first multiply 560 by the number of hanks (6) and divide by the ply number (2). 2ply worsted wool would have 1680 yards to a pound in weight. Coned yarns tend to be sold in multiples of 500g (approximately one pound); knowing the length of yarn on the cone can give you an indication of the thickness of yarn.

The metric system uses the same hank length of 1000 metres for all fibres and is concerned with the number of hanks to a kilogram in weight.

Other systems include the Denier system, used for man-made filament yarns and the International Tex system, both of which are based on units of weight by grams.

A good resource for learning about yarn counts: http://www.offtree.co.uk/converter/index.html

Societies, galleries and museums

British Fashion Council (UK)
www.britishfashioncouncil.com

Brooklyn Museum (USA)
www.brooklynmuseum.org

Costume Gallery (USA)
www.costumegallery.com

Costume Institute (USA)
www.metmuseum.org

Costume Society (UK)
www.costumesociety.org.uk

Council of Fashion Designers of
America (USA)
www.cfda.com

Crafts Council (UK)
www.craftscouncil.org.uk

Fashion and Textiles Museum (UK)
www.ftmlondon.org

Fashion Awareness Direct (UK)
www.fad.org.uk

Fashion Museum (UK)
www.museumofcostume.co.uk

Galleria del Costume (Italy)
www.polomuseale.firenze.it

Kobe Fashion Museum (Japan)
www.fashionmuseum.or.jp

Momu (Belgium)
www.momu.be

Musée de la Mode et du Costume de
la Ville de Paris (France)
www.lesartsdecoratifs.fr

Musèe des Arts de la mode (France)
www.lesartsdecoratifs.fr

Museum at the Fashion Institute of
Technology (USA)
www.fitnyc.edu

Museum Salvatore Ferragamo (Italy)
www.salvatoreferragamo.it

Prince's Trust (UK)
www.princes-trust.org.uk

Register of Apparel and Textile
Designers (UK)
www.yourcreativefuture.org.uk

Textile Institute (UK)
www.texi.org

V&A Museum (UK)
www.vam.ac.uk

The Worshipful Company of
Framework Knitters (UK)
www.agja63.dial.pipex.com

Websites

www.catwalking.com

www.craftcentral.org.uk

www.dazeddigital.com

www.designsponge.blogspot.com

www.ecca-london.org

www.edelkoort.com

www.fashioncapital.co.uk

www.fashion-enter.com

www.fashion-era.com

www.fashionoffice.org

www.gfw.org.uk

www.hintmag.com

www.knitkicks.co.uk

www.londonfashionweek.co.uk

www.loopknitting.com

www.marquise.de

www.premierevision.fr

www.promostyl.com

www.style.com

www.taitandstyle.co.uk

www.wgsn.com

Publications and magazines

10

Another Magazine

Arena Homme

Bloom

Collezioni

Dazed and Confused

Drapers Record

ID

International Textiles

Marmalade

Numero Magazine

Oyster

Pop

Selvedge

Tank

Textile View

View on Colour

Viewpoint

Visionaire

Designers

Alexander McQueeen

Bora Aksu

Christopher Kane

Clare Tough

Cooperative Designs

Craig Lawrence

Derek Lawlor

Hannah Buswell

Hannah Taylor

Issey Miyake

Johan Ku

Juliana Sissons

Julien McDonald

Mark Fast

Martin Margiela

Pandora Bahrami

Phoebe English

Pringle of Scotland

Rodarte

Sandra Backlund

Shao-Yen Chen

Shelley Fox

Sid Bryan

Simone Shailes

Sonia Rykiel

Victor and Rolf

Vivienne Westwood

Copley Marshall and Co Ltd
(Yarns)
Tunbridge Mills
Quay Street
Huddersfield
HD1 6QX
(No website)

The English Couture Company
(Interlinings and haberdashery)
18 The Green
High Street
Syston
Leicestershire
LE7 1HQ
www.englishcouture.co.uk

Fairfield Yarns
(Yarns)
9 Lea Mount Drive
Fairfield
Bury
Lancashire
BL9 7RR
www.fairfieldyarns.co.uk

Geoffrey E Macpherson Ltd
(Embroidery yarns, can be used for knit)
Unit 8 the Midway
Lenton
Nottingham
NG7 2TS
(No website)

George Weil Fibrecrafts
(Fibres, yarns and dyes)
Old Portsmouth Road
Peasmarsh
Guildford
Surrey
GU3 1LZ
www.fibrecrafts.com

The Handweavers' Studio and Gallery
(Fibres, yarns and equipment)
140 Seven Sisters Road
London
N7 7NS
www.handweavers.co.uk

Jamieson & Smith (Shetland Wool Brokers) Ltd
(Shetland yarns and fibres)
90 North Road
Lerwick
Shetland Islands
ZE1 0PQ
www.shetlandwoolbrokers.co.uk

John Andrews & Co.
(Linen yarns)
The Stables
51 Old Ballygowan Road
Comber
Newtownards
Co Down
BT23 5NP
www.andrewslinen.co.uk

The Lurex Company
(Metallic yarns)
1 Harewood Row
London
NW1 6SE
www.lurex.com

Scientific Wire Company
(Fine wire, suitable for knitting and weaving)
18 Raven Road
South Woodford
London
E18 1HW
www.scientificwire.com

Texere Yarns
(Yarns)
College Mill
Barkerend Road
Bradford
BD1 4AU
www.texere-yarns.co.uk

Todd and Duncan
(Cashmere yarns)
Lochleven Mills
Kinross
KY13 8DH
www.todd-duncan.com

Tortex Engineering
(Knitting machines and accessories)
Unit 8 Martlets Way
Goring-by-Sea
Worthing
BN12 4HF

Uppingham Yarns
(Yarns)
30 North Street East
Uppingham
Rutland
LE15 9QL
www.wools.co.uk

Whaleys (Bradford) Ltd
(Fabrics, interlinings and accessories)
Harris Court
Bradford
BD7 4EQ
www.whaleys-bradford.ltd.uk

Wingham Wool Work
(Fibres, yarns and dyes)
70 Main Street
Wentworth
Rotherham
S62 7TN
www.winghamwoolwork.co.uk

The Yarn Store
(Yarns)
17 Market Place
Oakham
Rutland
LE15 6DT
www.theyarnstore.co.uk

Yeoman Yarns
(Yarns)
36 Churchill Way
Fleckney
Leicestershire
LE8 8UD
www.yeoman-yarns.co.uk

Adanur S (1995)
**Wellington Sears handbook
of industrial textiles**
Technomic Pub.

Aldrich W (2004)
Metric pattern cutting
Blackwell

Allen J (1985)
The machine knitting book
Dorling Kindersley

Black S (2002)
Knitwear in fashion
Thames & Hudson

Brackenbury T (1992)
Knitted clothing technology
Blackwell Scientific Publications

Collier A M (1980)
A handbook of textiles
Wheaton

Compton R (1983)
**The complete book of
traditional knitting**
Batsford

Compton R (1986)
**The complete book of traditional
Guernsey and Jersey knitting**

Cooper J (2004)
**Textured knits: quick and
easy step-by-step projects**
Guild of Master Craftsman

Davis J (1982)
**Machine knitting to
suit your mood**
Pelham

Duberg A and van der Tol R (2008)
**Draping: art and craftsmanship
in fashion design**
De Jonge Hond

Faust R (1980)
**Fashion knit course outline
for hand-knitting machines**
Regine Studio

Foster L G (1922)
**Constructive and
decorative stitchery**
Educational Needlecraft Association

Foster V (2006)
Knitting handbook
Grange

Graham P (1988)
**The Hamlyn basic guide
to machine knitting**
Hamlyn

Gschwandtner S (2007)
**Knitknit: profiles + projects
from knitting's new wave**
Stewart, Tabori & Chang

Guagliumi S (1990)
**Machine knitting: hand tooling
techniques**
Batsford

Haffenden V (1997)
**Double bed machine knitting
explained**
University of Brighton

Hartley K M (1982)
Topics and questions in textiles
Heinemann Educational

Holbourne D (1979)
The book of machine knitting
Batsford

Hollingworth S (1982)
**The complete book of
traditional Aran knitting**
Batsford

Kiewe Heinz E (1971)
The sacred history of knitting
Art Needlework Industries

McGregor S (1981)
**The complete book of traditional
Fair Isle knitting**
Batsford

Mountford D (2000)
**The harmony guide to Aran
and Fair Isle knitting**
Collins & Brown

Musk D (1989)
**Machine knitting: the technique
of slipstitch**
Batsford

Musk D (1992)
**Machine knitting: technique
of pattern card design**
Batsford

Nabney J (1991)
**Designing garments on the
knitting machine**
Batsford

Rutt R (1987)
A history of hand knitting
Batsford

Shaeffer C B (1993)
Couture sewing techniques
Taunton

Sharp S (1986)
**Textured patterns for machine
knitting**
Batsford

Spencer D J (1989)
Knitting technology
Pergamon

Stanley H (1983)
**Modelling and flat cutting
for fashion**
Hutchinson

Tellier-Loumagne F (2005)
**The art of knitting: inspirational
stitches, textures and surfaces**
Thames & Hudson

Compiled by Indexing Specialists (UK) Ltd, Indexing House, 306A Portland Road, Hove, East Sussex BN3 6LP. Tel: 01273 416777. email: indexers@indexing.co.uk Website: www.indexing.co.uk

Acknowledgements

I would like to thank everyone who has supported me during this project, in particular to all the talented designers and to the students who have graduated from the University of Brighton, Northbrook College Sussex, London College of Fashion and the Royal College of Art. Your contributions of fantastic design and portfolio work have made this book what it is.

Thank you also to Janet Tong, who assisted with my research in the beginning and to Caterina Radvan for her help and support. I would especially like to thank Vikki Haffenden and Toni Hicks from the University of Brighton for their wonderful advice and continuing support throughout. Thank you also to Mark Hawdon and Sarah Elwick for all your help. A huge thank you to Tom Embleton and Jude Woodward from Northbrook College Sussex for their generous help and support.

A special thank you also to my dear friends Elizabeth Owen and Gina Ferri at Cosprop Ltd costumiers, London, who tirelessly helped source historical knitted garments when I was researching styles of knit and trim. Thank you to Shelley Fox for putting up with my endless request for images, thank you to Janet Sischgrund at Alexander McQueen for sourcing some beautiful images and thank you to Jojo Ma for introducing me to some very talented designers.

Of course, a very big thank you to Sifer Design and everyone at AVA, especially to my editor Rachel Netherwood for her amazing ability to keep patient under stress and mania (no more of my huge boxes of paper and disks cluttering up your office!). Thank you for a great learning curve.

Finally, thank you to my son, Tom Sissons, for typing up huge amounts of work and to my mum, dad and friends for listening to endless chat about the book. I can start socialising again now!

Picture credits

BASICS
FASHION DESIGN

Working with ethics

Lynne Elvins
Naomi Goulder

Publisher's note

The subject of ethics is not new, yet its consideration within the applied visual arts is perhaps not as prevalent as it might be. Our aim here is to help a new generation of students, educators and practitioners find a methodology for structuring their thoughts and reflections in this vital area.

AVA Publishing hopes that these **Working with ethics** pages provide a platform for consideration and a flexible method for incorporating ethical concerns in the work of educators, students and professionals. Our approach consists of four parts:

The **introduction** is intended to be an accessible snapshot of the ethical landscape, both in terms of historical development and current dominant themes.

The **framework** positions ethical consideration into four areas and poses questions about the practical implications that might occur. Marking your response to each of these questions on the scale shown will allow your reactions to be further explored by comparison.

The **case study** sets out a real project and then poses some ethical questions for further consideration. This is a focus point for a debate rather than a critical analysis so there are no predetermined right or wrong answers.

A selection of **further reading** for you to consider areas of particular interest in more detail.

Ethical: awareness/ reflection/ debate

Working with ethics

Introduction

Ethics is a complex subject that interlaces the idea of responsibilities to society with a wide range of considerations relevant to the character and happiness of the individual. It concerns virtues of compassion, loyalty and strength, but also of confidence, imagination, humour and optimism. As introduced in ancient Greek philosophy, the fundamental ethical question is *what should I do?* How we might pursue a 'good' life not only raises moral concerns about the effects of our actions on others, but also personal concerns about our own integrity.

In modern times the most important and controversial questions in ethics have been the moral ones. With growing populations and improvements in mobility and communications, it is not surprising that considerations about how to structure our lives together on the planet should come to the forefront. For visual artists and communicators it should be no surprise that these considerations will enter into the creative process.

Some ethical considerations are already enshrined in government laws and regulations or in professional codes of conduct. For example, plagiarism and breaches of confidentiality can be punishable offences. Legislation in various nations makes it unlawful to exclude people with disabilities from accessing information or spaces. The trade of ivory as a material has been banned in many countries. In these cases, a clear line has been drawn under what is unacceptable.

But most ethical matters remain open to debate, among experts and lay-people alike, and in the end we have to make our own choices on the basis of our own guiding principles or values. Is it more ethical to work for a charity than for a commercial company? Is it unethical to create something that others find ugly or offensive?

Specific questions such as these may lead to other questions that are more abstract. For example, is it only effects on humans (and what they care about) that are important, or might effects on the natural world require attention too?

Is promoting ethical consequences justified even when it requires ethical sacrifices along the way? Must there be a single unifying theory of ethics (such as the Utilitarian thesis that the right course of action is always the one that leads to the greatest happiness of the greatest number), or might there always be many different ethical values that pull a person in various directions?

As we enter into ethical debate and engage with these dilemmas on a personal and professional level, we may change our views or change our view of others. The real test though is whether, as we reflect on these matters, we change the way we act as well as the way we think. Socrates, the 'father' of philosophy, proposed that people will naturally do 'good' if they know what is right. But this point might only lead us to yet another question: *how do we know what is right?*

Working with ethics

You
What are your ethical beliefs?

Central to everything you do will be your attitude to people and issues around you. For some people their ethics are an active part of the decisions they make everyday as a consumer, a voter or a working professional. Others may think about ethics very little and yet this does not automatically make them unethical. Personal beliefs, lifestyle, politics, nationality, religion, gender, class or education can all influence your ethical viewpoint.

Using the scale, where would you place yourself? What do you take into account to make your decision? Compare results with your friends or colleagues.

Your client
What are your terms?

Working relationships are central to whether ethics can be embedded into a project and your conduct on a day-to-day basis is a demonstration of your professional ethics. The decision with the biggest impact is whom you choose to work with in the first place. Cigarette companies or arms traders are often-cited examples when talking about where a line might be drawn, but rarely are real situations so extreme. At what point might you turn down a project on ethical grounds and how much does the reality of having to earn a living affect your ability to choose?

Using the scale, where would you place a project? How does this compare to your personal ethical level?

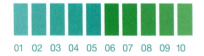

01 02 03 04 05 06 07 08 09 10

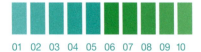

01 02 03 04 05 06 07 08 09 10

Your specifications
What are the impacts of your materials?

In relatively recent times we are learning that many natural materials are in short supply. At the same time we are increasingly aware that some man-made materials can have harmful, long-term effects on people or the planet. How much do you know about the materials that you use? Do you know where they come from, how far they travel and under what conditions they are obtained? When your creation is no longer needed, will it be easy and safe to recycle? Will it disappear without a trace? Are these considerations the responsibility of you or are they out of your hands?

Using the scale, mark how ethical your material choices are.

Your creation
What is the purpose of your work?

Between you, your colleagues and an agreed brief, what will your creation achieve? What purpose will it have in society and will it make a positive contribution? Should your work result in more than commercial success or industry awards? Might your creation help save lives, educate, protect or inspire? Form and function are two established aspects of judging a creation, but there is little consensus on the obligations of visual artists and communicators toward society, or the role they might have in solving social or environmental problems. If you want recognition for being the creator, how responsible are you for what you create and where might that responsibility end?

Using the scale, mark how ethical the purpose of your work is.

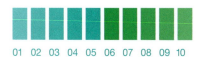

01 02 03 04 05 06 07 08 09 10

01 02 03 04 05 06 07 08 09 10

Working with ethics

One aspect of fashion design that raises an ethical dilemma is the way that clothes production has changed in terms of the speed of delivery of products and the now international chain of suppliers. 'Fast fashion' gives shoppers the latest styles sometimes just weeks after they first appeared on the catwalk, at prices that mean they can wear an outfit once or twice and then replace it. Due to lower labour costs in poorer countries, the vast majority of Western clothes are made in Asia, Africa, South America or Eastern Europe in potentially hostile and sometimes inhumane working conditions. It can be common for one piece of clothing to be made up of components from five or more countries, often thousands of miles apart, before they end up in the high-street store. How much responsibility should a fashion designer have in this situation if manufacture is controlled by retailers and demand is driven by consumers? Even if designers wish to minimise the social impact of fashion, what might they most usefully do?

Traditional Hawaiian feather capes (called *'Ahu'ula*) were made from thousands of tiny bird feathers and were an essential part of aristocratic regalia. Initially they were red (*'Ahu'ula* literally means 'red garment') but yellow feathers, being especially rare, became more highly prized and were introduced to the patterning.

The significance of the patterns, as well as their exact age or place of manufacture is largely unknown, despite great interest in their provenance in more recent times. Hawaii was visited in 1778 by English explorer Captain James Cook and feather capes were amongst the objects taken back to Britain.

The basic patterns are thought to reflect gods or ancestral spirits, family connections and an individual's rank or position in society. The base layer for these garments is a fibre net, with the surface made up of bundles of feathers tied to the net in overlapping rows. Red feathers came from the *'i'iwi* or the *'apapane*. Yellow feathers came from a black bird with yellow tufts under each wing called *'oo'oo*, or a *mamo* with yellow feathers above and below the tail.

Thousands of feathers were used to make a single cape for a high chief (the feather cape of King Kamehameha the Great is said to have been made from the feathers of around 80,000 birds). Only the highest-ranking chiefs had the resources to acquire enough feathers for a full-length cape, whereas most chiefs wore shorter ones which came to the elbow.

The demand for these feathers was so great that they acquired commercial value and provided a full-time job for professional feather-hunters. These fowlers studied the birds and caught them with nets or with bird lime smeared on branches. As both the 'i'iwi and 'apapane were covered with red feathers, the birds were killed and skinned. Other birds were captured at the beginning of the moulting season, when the yellow display feathers were loose and easily removed without damaging the birds.

The royal family of Hawaii eventually abandoned the feather cape as the regalia of rank in favour of military and naval uniforms decorated with braid and gold. The 'oo'oo and the mamo became extinct through the destruction of their forest feeding grounds and imported bird diseases. Silver and gold replaced red and yellow feathers as traded currency and the manufacture of feather capes became a largely forgotten art.

Is it more ethical to create clothing for the masses rather than for a few high-ranking individuals?

Is it unethical to kill animals to make garments?

Would you design and make a feather cape?

Fashion is a form of ugliness so intolerable that we have to alter it every six months.

Oscar Wilde

Working with ethics

AIGA
Design Business and Ethics
2007, AIGA

Eaton, Marcia Muelder
Aesthetics and the Good Life
1989, Associated University Press

Ellison, David
Ethics and Aesthetics in European Modernist Literature:
From the Sublime to the Uncanny
2001, Cambridge University Press

Fenner, David E W (Ed)
Ethics and the Arts:
An Anthology
1995, Garland Reference Library of Social Science

Gini, Al and Marcoux, Alexei M
Case Studies in Business Ethics
2005, Prentice Hall

McDonough, William and Braungart, Michael
Cradle to Cradle:
Remaking the Way We Make Things
2002, North Point Press

Papanek, Victor
Design for the Real World:
Making to Measure
1972, Thames and Hudson

United Nations Global Compact
The Ten Principles
www.unglobalcompact.org/AboutTheGC/TheTenPrinciples/index.html